Hope Without (

CW00549814

TERRY EAGLETON is Distinguish
Literature, University of Lancaster. He is the author of more
than fifty books spanning the fields of literary theory, postmod-
ernism, politics, ideology and religion, including the seminal
*Literary Theory: An Introduction. Eagleton's Culture, How to Read
Literature, Culture and the Death of God, The Event of Literature,
Why Marx Was Right, On Evil and Reason, Faith and Revolution* are
all published by Yale.

DAVID BEAN.

Hope Without Optimism

TERRY EAGLETON

YALE UNIVERSITY PRESS
NEW HAVEN AND LONDON

First published by the University of Virginia Press in 2015.

First published in paperback in 2017

For information about this and other Yale University Press publications please contact:
U.S. Office: sales.press@yale.edu   yalebooks.com
Europe Office: sales@yaleup.co.uk   yalebooks.co.uk

Typeset in Janson Text by IDSUK (DataConnection) Ltd
Printed in Great Britain by Hobbs The Printers, Totton, Hampshire

Library of Congress Control Number: 2015949374

ISBN 978-0-300-21712-4 (cloth)

ISBN 978-0-300-22644-7 (pbk)

10 9 8 7 6 5 4 3 2 1

For Nicholas Lash

We are not optimists; we do not present a lovely vision of the world which everyone is expected to fall in love with. We simply have, wherever we are, some small local task to do, on the side of justice, for the poor.

—Herbert McCabe, OP

Contents

Preface

As one for whom the proverbial glass is not only half empty but almost certain to contain some foul-tasting, potentially lethal liquid, I am not perhaps the most appropriate author to write about hope. There are those whose philosophy is 'eat, drink, and be merry, for tomorrow we die', and others, rather more congenial to my own taste, whose philosophy is 'tomorrow we die'. One reason why I have chosen to write on the subject despite these distressing proclivities is that it has been a curiously neglected notion in an age which, in Raymond Williams's words, confronts us with 'the felt loss of a future'.[1] Perhaps another reason for fighting shy of the subject is the fact that those who venture to speak of it are bound to find themselves languishing in the shadow of Ernst Bloch's monumental *The Principle of Hope*, a work which I discuss in chapter 3. Bloch's work may not be the most admirable in the annals of Western Marxism, but it is by far the longest.

Philosophers, it has been claimed, have largely abandoned hope. A cursory glance at a library catalogue suggests they have abjectly surrendered the subject to books with such titles as *Half Full: Forty Inspiring Stories of Optimism, Hope, and Faith*; *A Little Faith, Hope and Hilarity*; and (my personal favourite) *The Years of Hope: Cambridge, Colonial Administration in the South Seas and Cricket*, not to speak of numerous biographies of Bob Hope. It is a subject that seems to attract every dewy-eyed moralist and spiritual cheerleader on the planet. There is room, then, for a reflection on the topic from one like myself who has a background neither in cricket nor in colonial administration, but who is interested in the political, philosophical, and theological implications of the idea.

This book grew out of the Page-Barbour Lectures at the University of Virginia, which I was invited to deliver in 2014. I am deeply grateful to all those in Charlottesville who made me feel welcome during my stay there, and especially to Jenny Geddes. I must record my particular gratitude to Chad Wellmon, who organised my visit with superb efficiency and proved himself a most congenial and conscientious host.

T.E.

1

The Banality of Optimism

THERE MAY BE many good reasons for believing that a situation will turn out well, but to expect that it will do so because you are an optimist is not one of them. It is just as irrational as believing that all will be well because you are an Albanian, or because it has just rained for three days in a row. If there is no good reason why things should work out satisfactorily, there is no good reason why they should not turn out badly either, so that the optimist's belief is baseless. It is possible to be a pragmatic optimist, in the sense of feeling assured that this problem, but not that one, will be resolved; but what one might call a professional or card-carrying optimist feels sanguine about specific situations because he or she tends to feel sanguine in general. He will find his lost nose stud or inherit a Jacobean manor house because life as a whole is not so bad. He is thus in danger of buying his hope on the cheap. In fact, there is a sense in which optimism is more a matter of belief than of hope. It is based on an opinion that things tend to work out well, not on the strenuous commitment that hope involves. Henry James thought it rife in both life and letters. 'As for the aberrations of a shallow optimism', he writes in 'The Art of Fiction', 'the ground (of English fiction especially) is strewn with their brittle particles as with broken glass.'[1]

Optimism as a general outlook is self-sustaining.[2] If it is hard to argue against, it is because it is a primordial stance toward the world, like cynicism or credulity, which lights up the facts from its own peculiar angle and is thus resistant to being refuted by them. Hence the hackneyed metaphor of seeing the world through rose-tinted spectacles, which will colour whatever might challenge your vision with the same ruddy glow. In a kind of moral astigmatism, one skews the truth to fit one's natural proclivities, which have already taken all the vital decisions on your behalf. Since pessimism involves much the same kind of spiritual kink, the two moods have more in common than is generally thought. The psychologist Erik Erikson speaks of a 'maladaptive optimism' whereby the infant fails to acknowledge the bounds of the possible by failing to register the desires of those around it, and their incompatibility with its own.[3] Recognising the intransigence of reality is in Erikson's view vital to the formation of the ego, but it is just this that the chronic or professional optimist finds hard to achieve.

An optimist is not just someone with high hopes. Even a pessimist can feel positive on a particular issue, whatever his or her habitual gloom. One can have hope without feeling that things in general are likely to turn out well. An optimist is rather someone who is bullish about life simply because he is an optimist. He anticipates congenial conclusions because this is the way it is with him. As such, he fails to take the point that one must have reasons to be happy.[4] Unlike hope, then, professional optimism is not a virtue, any more than having freckles or flat feet is a virtue. It is not a disposition one attains through deep reflection or disciplined study. It is simply a quirk of temperament. 'Always look on the bright side of life' has about as much rational force as 'always part your hair in the middle', or 'always tip your hat obsequiously to an Irish wolfhound'.

The equally moth-eaten image of the glass which is half full or half empty depending on one's viewpoint is instructive in this respect. The image betrays the fact that there is nothing in the situation itself to determine one's response to it. It can offer no challenge to your habitual prejudices. There is nothing objectively at stake. You will see the same amount of liquid whether you are of a carefree or morose turn of mind. How one feels about the glass, then, is purely arbitrary. And whether a judgment that is purely arbitrary can be said to be a judgment at all is surely doubtful.

There can certainly be no arguing over the matter, as for the more epistemologically naive forms of postmodernism there can be no arguing over beliefs. The fact is that you see the world in your way and I see it in mine, and there is no neutral ground on which these two points of view might enter into mutual contention. Since any such ground would itself be interpreted differently by the viewpoints in question, it would not be neutral at all. Neither standpoint can be empirically disproved, since each will interpret the facts in a way that confirms its own validity. In a similar way, both optimism and pessimism are forms of fatalism. There is nothing you can do about being an optimist, rather as there is nothing you can do about being five foot four. You are chained to your cheerfulness like a slave to his oar, a glum enough prospect. All that is really possible, then, as with epistemological relativism, is for the two camps to respect each other's opinion in a rather toothless kind of tolerance. There are no rational grounds for deciding between these cases, any more than for a certain strain of moral relativism are there rational grounds for deciding between inviting your friends to dinner and hanging them upside down from the rafters while you rifle their pockets. Authentic hope, by contrast, needs to be underpinned by reasons. In this, it resembles love, of which theologically speaking it is a specific mode. It must be able to pick out the features of a situation that render it credible. Otherwise it is just a gut feeling, like being convinced that there is an octopus under your bed. Hope must be fallible, as temperamental cheerfulness is not.

Even when optimism acknowledges that the facts do not support it, its ebullience can remain undented. Mark Tapley, a character in Charles Dickens's *Martin Chuzzlewit*, is so fanatically good-humoured that he seeks out the kind of dire situations that would drive others to despair, so as to demonstrate that his geniality is not bought on the cheap. Since Tapley wants his circumstances to be as distressing as possible in order to feel satisfied with himself, his optimism is actually a form of egoism, as are most points of view in the novel. It is akin to sentimentalism, another form of congeniality which is secretly about itself. Self-ishness is so rife in *Martin Chuzzlewit* that even Tapley's gener-osity of spirit is portrayed as a kind of idiosyncrasy or a quirk of temperament, scarcely a moral phenomenon at all. There is a sense in which he does not really want his situation to improve, since this would rob his heartiness of its moral worth. His jovial disposition is thus complicit with the forces that spread misery around him. The pessimist is similarly suspicious of efforts at improvement—not because they would deprive him of opportu-nities for jolliness, but because he believes that they are almost certain to fail.

Optimists tend to believe in progress. But if things can be im-proved, then it follows that their present condition leaves some-thing to be desired. In this sense, optimism is not quite as bullish as what the eighteenth century knew as optimalism – the Leib-nizian doctrine that we inhabit the best of all possible worlds. Optimism is not as optimistic as optimalism. For the optimalist, we already enjoy the best of all possible cosmic arrangements; the optimist, by contrast, may acknowledge the shortcomings of the present while looking to a more lustrous future. It is a question of whether perfection is here already, or whether it is a goal to-wards which we are heading. It is not hard, however, to see how optimalism can constitute a recipe for moral inertia, which might then undercut its claim that the world cannot be improved on.

Optimalists are as bereft of hope as nihilists because they have no need of it. Since they see no call for change, they may find themselves in league with those conservatives for whom such change is deplorable, or for whom our condition is too corrupt to allow of it. Henry James remarks that 'although a conservative is not necessarily an optimist, I think an optimist is pretty likely to be a conservative'.[5] Optimists are conservatives because their faith in a benign future is rooted in their trust in the essential soundness of the present. Indeed, optimism is a typical compo-nent of ruling-class ideologies. If governments do not generally encourage their citizens to believe that there is some frightful apocalypse lurking around the corner, it is partly because the alternative to a bright-eyed citizenry may be political disaffection. Bleakness, by contrast, can be a radical posture. Only if you view your situation as critical do you recognise the need to transform it. Dissatisfaction can be a goad to reform. The sanguine, by contrast, are likely to come up with sheerly cosmetic solutions. True hope is needed most when the situation is at its starkest, a state of extremity that optimism is generally loath to acknowledge. One would prefer not to have to hope, since the need to do so is a sign that the unpalatable has already happened. For the Hebrew scriptures, for example, hope has a gloomy subtext, involving as it does the confounding of the ungodly. If one has need of the virtue, it is because there are a great many villains around.

Friedrich Nietzsche distinguishes in *Schopenhauer as Educator* between two kinds of cheerfulness – one inspired by a tragic confrontation with the terrible, as with the ancient Greeks, and a shallow brand of heartiness which buys its buoyancy at the expense of an awareness of the irreparable. It is unable to look the monsters it purports to combat squarely in the eyes. To this extent, hope and temperamental optimism are at daggers drawn. True lightness of spirit in Nietzsche's view is arduous, exacting, a question of courage and self-overcoming. It dismantles the distinction between joy and seriousness, which is why he can write in *Ecce Homo* of being 'cheerful among nothing but hard truths'. Nietzsche had, to be sure, disreputable reasons for rejecting optimism as well. In *The Birth of Tragedy* he dismisses it in macho spirit as a 'weakling doctrine', and associates it with the dangerous revolutionary aspirations of the 'slave class' of his day.

Theodor Adorno once observed that those thinkers who give us the sober, unvarnished truth (he had Freud in particular in mind) were of more service to humanity than the wide-eyed utopianists. We shall be seeing later how Adorno's colleague Walter Benjamin built his revolutionary vision on a distrust of historical progress, as well as on a profound melancholia. Benjamin himself calls this outlook 'pessimism', but one might equally see it as realism, that most difficult of moral conditions to attain. In a celebrated essay on surrealism, he speaks of the urgent need to 'organise' pessimism for political ends, countering the facile optimism of certain sectors of the left. There is, he writes, a need for 'pessimism all along the line. Absolutely. Mistrust of the fate of literature, mistrust of the fate of freedom, mistrust of the fate of European humanity, but three times mistrust of all reconciliation between classes, between nations, between individuals. And unlimited trust only in I. G. Farben and the peaceful perfection of the air force.'[6] Benjamin's dogged scepticism is in the service of human welfare. It is an attempt to remain coldly unmystified for the sake of constructive action. In other hands, to be sure, this despondent vision might call the very possibility of political transformation into question. Perhaps a certain impotence belongs to the general cataclysm. If this is so, then the worse your condition grows, the harder it may be to alter. This is not Benjamin's view. For him, the refutation of optimism is an essential condition of political change.

Optimism and pessimism can be features of worldviews as well as of individuals. Liberals, for example, tend to the former, while conservatives incline to the latter. Generally speaking, the liberal trusts that men and women will conduct themselves decently if they are allowed to flourish freely, whereas the conservative tends to see them as flawed, wayward creatures who must be curbed and disciplined if anything profitable is to be squeezed out of them. There is a similar distinction between Romantics and classicists. The Middle Ages were by and large less euphoric in their estimation of humankind than the Renaissance, sunk as they were in a sense of sin and corruption. Ignatius Reilly, hero of John Kennedy Toole's novel *A Confederacy of Dunces* and a staunch champion of medieval civilisation, declares that 'optimism nauseates me. It is perverse. Since man's fall, his proper position in the universe has been one of misery.'

Conservatives tend to divide between so-called deteriorationists, for whom there was a golden age from which we have calamitously lapsed, and those for whom every age is as degenerate as every other. It is possible to read T. S. Eliot's *The Waste Land* as combining these mutually contradictory cases. There were also those late-nineteenth-century ideologues who were upbeat and downbeat at the same time, hymning the virtues of civility and technology while seeing them as everywhere coupled with entropy and degradation, not least in the spawning of a semi-bestial underclass.[7] Both Marxists and Christians are gloomier about the current condition of humanity than liberals and social reformists, yet far more hopeful about its future prospects. In both cases, these two attitudes are sides of the same coin. One has faith in the future precisely because one seeks to confront the present at its most rebarbative. It is, as we shall see later, a tragic way of seeing, foreign alike to sunny progressivists and grim-faced Jeremiahs.

That there has indeed been progress in the history of humanity can scarcely be doubted.[8] Those who do take leave to doubt it, a group which includes a number of postmodern thinkers, have presumably no wish to revert to witch-burning, a slave-owning economy, twelfth-century sanitation, or pre-anaesthetic surgery. That we live in a world rattling with nuclear weapons and scarred by spectacular poverty is no refutation of the truth that some things have grown unimaginably better. What is in question is not progress but Progress. To believe that there is progress in history is not necessarily to believe that history as such is climbing upward. At their most sanguine and self-admiring, the middle classes of an earlier epoch held that humanity was evolving under its own steam toward a higher, perhaps even utopian state. So-called perfectibilism ranked among the convictions of otherwise hard-nosed, pragmatic scientists and politicians. We shall be looking later at a left-wing version of this faith in the writings of Ernst Bloch. One might describe this outlook (though not in Bloch's case) as optimistic fatalism – a curious conjuncture, to be sure, since fatalism in our own time is more usually to be found in the company of pessimism. The inevitable is generally unpleasant. Whereas the glass-half-full image reduces hope to pure subjectivity, the doctrine of progress reifies it to an objective reality. Humanity for the likes of Herbert Spencer and Auguste Comte can cooperate with the mighty laws that drive history onward and upward, or it can obstruct them; but it is powerless to alter their fundamental nature, any more than one could tinker with Providence. Much the same goes for Immanuel Kant, for whom Nature itself guarantees a future of perpetual peace, but does so through such free human activities as trade and commerce. Hope, so to speak, is built into the structure of reality itself. It is as much an innate feature of the world as the forces that shape the anatomy of the starfish. Even if we forget about it, it will not forget about us. It is a view that risks reducing men and women to political torpor, since if a glorious future is assured, it is hard to see why they should stir themselves to strive for it. The kind of Marxism for which a communist future is copper-bottomed needs to explain why it also has to be struggled for.

Extravagant forms of optimism can be morally dubious. Among them is theodicy, the attempt to justify evil on the grounds that good may come from it, which raises end-of-pier optimism to cosmic status. For Alexander Pope's *Essay on Man*, a poem that owes a heavy debt to Leibniz and deism, evil is simply good misapprehended. If we were able to view rape and slavery from the standpoint of the universe as a whole, we would recognise the essential part they play in the general well-being. Moral protest is really myopia. As a character in Georg Büchner's play *Danton's Death* speculates, 'There is an ear for which the riotous cacophony which deafens us is but a stream of harmonies.' Besides, misery can make a man of you. God, writes the philosopher Richard Swinburne, is justified in allowing 'Hiroshima, Belsen, the Lisbon Earthquake or the Black Death' so that men and women can live in a real world rather than a toy one.[9] Toy worlds do not present us with stiff enough challenges, and thus yield us scant chance to flex our moral muscles. It is hard to imagine anyone but an academic proposing such a case.

Theodicies of this offensively hard-nosed kind do not teach

that evil, however repugnant in itself, may occasionally give birth to good, a case difficult to deny, but that it should be accepted or even embraced as a necessary condition of such value. The problem for some Enlightenment thinkers of this persuasion was that the more the universe appeared a rational, harmonious whole, the larger loomed the problem of evil.[10] Such cosmic optimism tends to be self-defeating, since it throws into relief what it finds hardest to accommodate. Those who believe in perfectibility are more likely to be appalled by the prospect of war and genocide than the cynics and misanthropes, who might find in such misfortunes consoling evidence that they were right about human degeneracy all along.

There were those in the eighteenth century who denied the reality of evil, while some in the nineteenth century held that the problem it posed could be resolved by the doctrine of progress. The deist vision could be historicised. Evil was real enough, but it was en route to being eradicated. The notion of progress thus allowed one to acknowledge the undeniable while retaining one's faith in human perfection. For a certain historicist vision, drudgery and deprivation could be justified by the role they played in the general enhancement of the species. Without backbreaking toil for some, no civilised existence for others. For every great sculpture or symphony, a row of wretched hovels. That there is no civilised existence without exploitation was a view held by Friedrich Nietzsche, as well as by a good many others less brazenly prepared to proclaim it. Labour is the progenitor of culture, and like a downtrodden parent finds solace for its afflictions in the success of its offspring. For its part, culture shows all the reluctance to acknowledge its shabby parentage of a superstar from the back streets.

If the ideologues of early capitalism had hope, it was among other things because they did not regard their system as self-complete. Production was a chronicle still to be consummated. Late capitalism, by contrast, is considerably less hopeful, which is not to say that it is dispirited. The consumerist self, unlike the productivist one, inhabits this or that serialised moment of time rather than anything resembling a narrative. It is too random and diffuse to be the subject of an intelligible evolution. There is thus no radically altered future to look to. Hope on a sizeable scale is accordingly superannuated. Nothing world-historical is likely to happen again, since the space in which it might occur has crumbled to dust. The future will simply be an endlessly distended present. One can thus combine the excitement of seeing what futurity will deliver with the comfort of knowing that it will involve no inconvenient upheaval. In an earlier era of capitalism, one could be hopeful because one could foresee a resplendent future; in a later stage of the same system, what meagre expectancy there is lies in the assumption that the future will be a reprise of the present. There is not much hope around; but this itself is a hopeful sign, since it means that there is nothing to be redeemed.[11]

Nations, like political creeds, can be upbeat or downbeat. Along with North Korea, the United States is one of the few countries on earth in which optimism is almost a state ideology. For large sectors of the nation, to be bullish is to be patriotic, while negativity is a species of thought crime. Pessimism is thought to be vaguely subversive. Even in the most despondent of times, a collective fantasy of omnipotence and infinity continues to haunt the national unconscious. It would be almost as impossible to elect a US president who advised the nation that its best days were behind it as it would be to elect a chimpanzee, though as far as that goes there have been one or two near misses. Any such leader would be a prime target for assassination. An American historian remarked recently that 'presidential inaugural speeches are always optimistic whatever the times'. The comment was not intended as a criticism. There is a compulsive cheeriness about some aspects of American culture, an I-can-do-anything-I-want rhetoric which betrays a quasi-pathological fear of failure.

In an excruciatingly styleless study entitled *The Biology of Hope*, the Canadian scholar Lionel Tiger, anxious to place his country's ideology of hope on a scientific basis, is much preoccupied with drugged monkeys, mood-altering substances, and chemical changes found in the excretion of parents grieving for their dead children. If only one could search out the physiological basis of joviality, it might be possible to eradicate political disaffection and ensure a permanently ecstatic citizenry. Hope is a politically useful stimulant. 'The possibility exists', Tiger comments, 'that it is a common human obligation to augment optimism.'[12] Stalin and Mao seem to have held much the same view. It is our moral duty to insist that all is well, even when it self-evidently isn't.

In a similar vein, the authors of a work entitled *Hope in the Age of Anxiety* inform us that 'hopefulness is the best medicine because it represents an adaptive middle ground between the overactivated stress response and the disengaged giving-up complex'. Hope assures us of 'appropriate levels of neurotransmitters, hormones, lymphocytes, and other critical health-related substances'.[13] A deficiency of the stuff is bad for your personal and political health. Perhaps there are already scientists in California at work on converting it into tablet form. The American philosopher William James was restive with this saccharine vision. 'Is the last word sweet?' he asks. 'Is all "yes, yes" in the universe? Doesn't the fact of "no" stand at the very core of life? Doesn't the very "seriousness" that we attribute to life mean that ineluctable noes and losses form a part of it, that there are genuine sacrifices somewhere, and that something permanently drastic and bitter always remains at the bottom of the cup?'[14]

The 'faith-based' rather than 'reality-based' politics of the George W. Bush White House pressed a familiar American attitude to the point of lunacy. Reality is a pessimist to whose treasonable talk one must shut one's ears. Since the truth is often enough unpleasant, it must be trumped by the unflinching will. It is a vein of optimism not easy to distinguish from mental illness. Cheerfulness of this kind is a form of psychological disavowal. For all its square-jawed vigour, it is really a moral evasion. It is the enemy of hope, which is necessary precisely because one is able to confess how grave a situation is. By contrast, the jauntiness that causes the optimist to hope also leads him to underestimate the obstacles to tackling it, and thus to end up with a fairly worthless kind of assurance. Optimism does not take despair seriously enough. The emperor Franz Joseph is reputed to have remarked that whereas in Berlin things were serious but not hopeless, in Vienna they were hopeless but not serious.

Cheeriness is one of the most banal of emotions. One associates it with cavorting around in a striped jacket and red plastic nose. The very word 'happiness', as opposed to the French *bonheur* or the ancient Greek *eudaemonia*, has chocolate-box connotations, while 'contentment' has too bovine a ring. 'A man of no understanding', writes the author of the Book of Ecclesiastes, 'has vain and false hope.' The French philosopher Gabriel Marcel doubts that there can be any deep optimism.[15] Perhaps it is best seen as a degenerate, incorrigibly naive form of hope. There is something intolerably brittle about it, as there can be something morbidly self-indulgent about a pessimism that feeds with thinly disguised glee off its own glumness. Like pessimism, optimism spreads a monochrome glaze over the whole world, blind to nuance and distinction. Since it is a general mind-set, all objects become blandly interchangeable, in a kind of exchange value of the spirit. The card-carrying optimist responds to everything in the same rigorously preprogrammed way, and so eliminates chance and contingency. In this deterministic world, things are destined with preternatural predictability to work out well, and for no good reason whatsoever.

It is a remarkable fact that between the appearance of Samuel Richardson's *Clarissa* in the mid-eighteenth century and the fiction of Thomas Hardy in late Victorian England there is scarcely a tragic novel (in the sense of one with a calamitous ending) to be found. There are, to be sure, a few hair-raisingly near misses. *Wuthering Heights* sails close to the brink of tragedy, while Charlotte Brontë's *Villette* presents the reader with alternative endings, one tragic and one comic, as though nervous of closing entirely on the former note. Maggie Tulliver, the protagonist of George Eliot's *The Mill on the Floss*, dies at the end of the narrative, but in such ecstatic union with her stiff-necked churl of a brother that the conclusion is curiously uplifting. Though Eliot's

Middlemarch ends on a muted note, it affirms its faith in the reforming spirit, however sombrely qualified, in its final breath. The final words of Dickens's *Little Dorrit* are fairly comfortless, but the novel, like all of its author's works, refuses to press its disenchantment through to outright tragedy. True to this impulse, Dickens altered the ending of *Great Expectations* to bring its hero and heroine together. Even when it is portraying the grimmest of social realities, at least in the earlier fiction, his pyrotechnic style places them enjoyably at arm's length. The verve and brio with which he depicts the most harrowing features of Victorian England is itself a way of surmounting them.

If Thomas Hardy scandalised some of his readers, it was less because of his atheism or enlightened sexual opinions than his unswerving tragic realism. It was his refusal of fictional as well as religious consolation, of opiates of one kind or another, that proved so disquieting to a Victorian audience sorely in need of fictional consolation. Tess Durbeyfield and Jude Fawley are fully fledged tragic protagonists, and as such strikingly unfamiliar figures in the annals of English fiction. Samuel Richardson turned a deaf ear to the pleas of the distressed gentlefolk who were anxiously following the fortunes of his heroine Clarissa that he should come to her rescue, choosing instead to press the action obdurately through to her death. If the Victorians were especially disconcerted by dejection, it was not least because gloom was felt to be socially disruptive. In an age of social turmoil, one of art's primary purposes was to edify. The point of fiction, as Freud argues of fantasy in general, was to correct the blunders of an unsatisfying reality. The English novel lent support to the status quo not only in its respect for rank or regard or social order but also in its relentless insistence on upbeat endings.

Even in our own disenchanted days, writers of dust-jacket copy regularly try to discern glimmers of hope in the darkest of fictions, presumably on the assumption that readers are likely to find excessive despondency too dispiriting. Even so, we are accustomed to our narratives ending on a cheerless or inconclusive note. When they fail to be suitably downbeat, the effect can be arresting. Such is the case with José Saramago's novel *Blindness*, at the conclusion of which a group of men and women who have inexplicably lost their eyesight have their vision just as abruptly restored. One by one, these sightless characters pass through their darkness into the light. For a contemporary piece of fiction to end on such a joyfully transformative note is almost as audacious as if *Pride and Prejudice* were to conclude with a massacre of the Bennet sisters.

There are those for whom optimism, while not exactly deep, is at least rational. Matt Ridley's stylish, erudite *The Rational Optimist* differs from end-of-pier cavorting in basing its sprightly vision of the world on what it sees as the facts. It also offers us this magnificently angry paragraph:

> Even after the best half-century for poverty reduction, there are still hundreds of millions going blind for lack of vitamin A in their monotonous diet, or watching their children's bellies swell from protein deficiency, or awash with preventable dysentery caused by contaminated water, or coughing with avoidable pneumonia caused by the smoke of indoor fires, or wasting from treatable AIDS, or shivering with unnecessary malaria. There are people living in hovels of dried mud, slums of corrugated iron, or towers of soulless concrete (including the 'Africas within' the West), people who never get a chance to read a book or see a doctor. There are young boys who carry machine guns and young girls who sell their bodies. If my great grand-daughter reads this book in 2200 I want her to know that I am acutely aware of the inequality of the world I inhabit, a world where I can worry about my weight and a restaurant owner can moan about the iniquity of importing green beans by air from Kenya in winter, while in Darfur a child's shrunken face is covered in flies, in Somalia a woman is stoned to death and in Afghanistan a lone American entrepreneur builds schools while his government drops bombs.[16]

It is hardly a Panglossian vision. On the contrary, it is a moving, passionate *cri de coeur*, of remarkable eloquence and compassion. Despite his outrage, however, Ridley regards the modern age as a chronicle of stupendous progress, and he is surely right to do so. Generally speaking, human beings are richer, freer, taller, healthier, more peaceable, more mobile, better educated, more leisurely, secure and comfortable than at any previous time in their violent, diseased, poverty-stricken history. Ridley would no doubt be bemused to learn that Karl Marx would have heartily endorsed his view. In fact, there are times when one wonders whether this former chairman of a spectacularly failed bank is a Marxist in pinstripe clothing, not least given his faith in the steady unfolding of the productive forces. It is just that whereas Ridley sees a direct relation between material affluence and human well-being, Marx harbours no such mechanistic illusions. It is true that the former is a necessary condition of the latter, since only saints can flourish when they are starving, but it is not a sufficient one. By and large, *The Rational Optimist* overlooks this fact, indulging from time to time in the kind of crude technological determinism that would cause any self-respecting Marxist to wince. The sexual liberation of women, for example, is directly attributed to 'labour-saving electrical machinery' (108). Liberty and human welfare, so we are admonished, march hand in hand with trade and prosperity. The fact that trade and prosperity have also marched hand in hand with slavery, sweatshops, political despotism and colonialist genocide is prudently passed over.

All the same, Marx would agree that modernity has been an exhilarating tale of progress, prosperity and emancipation. The myth of the noble savage, of which Ridley is properly disdainful, earned his contempt as well. The one sure fact about the so-called organic society, as Raymond Williams once remarked, is that it has always gone.[17] Marx's outlook, however, is rather more nuanced than Ridley's. Whereas Ridley sees the modern age as a runaway success story marred by certain residual pockets of deprivation, Marx not only regards it as a tale of triumph and horror together but sees these two narratives as tightly interwoven.

In his view, the very forces that make for freedom and affluence also lay waste human powers, generate inequality and impoverishment, and hold despotic sway over human lives. There can be no civilisation without barbarism, no cathedrals or corporations without drudgery and the fear of destitution. Humanity's problem is not simply a lack of power or resources, but the very capabilities it has so magnificently evolved. It is hubris that threatens it, not simply backwardness. If history is a record of human advance, it is also a nightmare weighing on the brains of the living.

If Marx is a Pangloss, then, he is also a Jeremiah. Ridley's outlook, by contrast, is at once more innocent and more simplistic. There is a vein of embarrassing naïveté within his worldly-wiseness. Whereas Marx sees an emancipatory potential in markets, exchange value and the global circulation of commodities, Ridley, to whom this fact would no doubt come as a surprise, tends to see nothing else. Whatever concessions he may make to the shrunken faces of the children of Darfur, his outlook is drastically one-sided. A judicious apologist for market forces would point to their role in the rapid accumulation of wealth, as well as in the general advance of global civilisation, while acknowledging that this has involved not only poverty and inequality but a crassly instrumental rationality, ruthless acquisitiveness, economic instability, selfish individualism, destructive military adventures, the withering of social and civic bonds, pervasive cultural banality, and the philistine erasure of the past. Such an apologist might concede all or some of these points while insisting that capitalism outmatches any other economic system in its efficiency and productivity; that socialism has proved a disaster in practice; and that some of the most baneful features of the current system might be regulated or reformed.

Ridley, however, is complacently silent about almost all of these unpalatable aspects of the system he champions, not least about the imperialist warfare to which it regularly gives rise. For him, these are the sour-faced caveats of those for whom modernity simply means decline. Yet they are also the views of Marx and his epigones, all of them advocates of technology and enthusiasts of human advancement. *The Communist Manifesto* rivals *The Rational Optimist* in its admiration for free markets, capitalist innovation and a globalised economy. It is simply that it also reckons the atrocious costs of these gains, as the supposedly reality-based Ridley does not.

Ridley regards his own optimism as rational because it is rooted in reality. Far from being a dispassionate judge, however, he is an embattled ideologue who sifts the facts for those most likely to reinforce his case. One such example is his astonishingly cavalier treatment of the danger of nuclear war, on which the book expends no less than an entire paragraph. Nuclear weapons, Ridley admits, posed a genuine threat during the Cold War, and the perils of nuclear conflict are far from having faded; but a great many such armaments have been dismantled, and the general impression the book gives is that we can afford to stop fussing. Nuclear missiles would seem to be as much Cold War memorabilia as Doris Day or drainpipe trousers. This is red-nosed euphoria with a vengeance. The embarrassment such weapons present for progressivists, needless to say, is that humanity can forge ahead only if it is still present on the planet to do so. The nonexistence of the species poses an even graver problem for the march of progress than those who spend their spare time dressing up as Regency dandies. Having always possessed the power to annihilate ourselves individually, we have now advanced with admirable technological ingenuity to the point of being able to accomplish this end collectively. Suicide, so to speak, has been socialised, taken into public ownership. As the Polish author Stanisław Lec comments, 'It would be a laugh if they didn't finish up ending the world before the end of the world.'[18] There is no more abundant testimony to one's sovereign power than the capacity to destroy oneself. The suicide, remarks a character in a Dostoevsky novel, becomes for a brief moment a god, able to dispose of his own life with divine omnipotence.

Human beings have always lived in dread of some fearful apocalypse; what they failed to reckon with until recently was the possibility that this cosmic catastrophe might prove to be of their own inventing. Ridley, however, remains unmoved by the prospect of the species bringing down the curtain on its own less-than-enthralling performance. His procedure is to list a number of grave threats to humanity (famine, plague, environmental disaster and so on), only to point out with a flourish of satisfaction that they haven't happened yet, or that the risk of them has notably diminished. This is rather like boasting in 1913 that there had never been a world war, or that a calamitous viral epidemic was out of the question. Whatever else one might dub such optimism, 'rational' is most certainly a misnomer. Ridley hasn't died yet either, but he would be unwise to draw too comforting a conclusion from the fact.

The Rational Optimist is right to sing the virtues of barter, trade, exchange, technology, the division of labour, pooled inventiveness and the swapping of bright ideas. It is through such activities that humanity has become a truly universal species. For Marx, too, an author who is always prepared to give the devil his due, these features of human history represent a veritable quantum leap out of poverty and parochialism. It is just that he is also alert to the destructive effects of such global interconnectedness, as the relentlessly tunnel-visioned Ridley is not. That Ridley fails to note such effects comes as something of a surprise, given that he was formerly non-executive chairman of Northern Rock, the bank at the vortex of the British financial meltdown of 2008. Indeed, it is testimony to his unswerving conviction in this respect that he quotes admiringly from an economist who maintains that 'societies that use markets extensively develop a culture of co-operation, fairness and respect for the individual' (86). When it comes to a faith in the hidden hand of the market, Ridley makes Adam Smith look like Joseph Stalin. Individual acts of selfishness, however sordid, will always be alchemised into overall achievement. Apparently unperturbed by one squalid revelation of fraud, greed, barefaced deception and criminal malpractice after another, he is even able to assure us that 'the more people are immersed in the collective brain of the modern commercial world, the more generous they are' (86). The market, he assures us, 'gives a vast reason for optimism about the future of the human race' (10), given that it 'can turn many individually selfish motives into a collectively kind result' (105). The fact that it can also spawn calamitous consequences is tactfully suppressed, despite Ridley's intimate personal acquaintance with this phenomenon. The countless men and women who were robbed of their homes and savings by swindling financiers, and who were then forced to foot the bill for their cupidity, would doubtless take leave to query such claims. Trust in the capitalist financial system has actually grown, Ridley informs us, writing as he does at a point when many of the world's citizens regard bankers with only slightly less revulsion than they do paedophiles or giant squids.

Slavery and child labour, Ridley proudly points out, were outlawed in the nineteenth century. He fails to add that almost every enlightened measure of this kind was achieved in the teeth of ferocious resistance from the very social system he acclaims. Racism, sexism and child molestation, he argues, have today become unacceptable. The fact that they are still to be found everywhere one turns seems a minor detail by comparison. So unshakeable is his faith in progress that he is even prepared to look with a certain equanimity on the collapse of much of the globe. Even if Europe, America and the Islamic world go to the wall, China, he insists, would surely keep the torch of progress alight. The roseate future of the species, in other words, is in the hands of a brutally autocratic state.

Ridley may not be even-handed, but he is certainly self-contradictory. He celebrates capitalism, but drapes the term in scare quotes and suggests that it is about to disappear. He means by this that the Victorian version has given way to the post-industrial one, but it suits his case better to cast doubt on the system's very existence. Somewhat disarmingly, he concedes that the world will end in disaster if we carry on the way we do, while clinging stubbornly to the prospect of a radiant future. 'The wrong kind of chiefs, priests and thieves', he acknowledges, 'could yet snuff out future prosperity on earth' (358), despite insisting elsewhere that they won't. In Micawberish spirit, Ridley has an unquenchable belief that something will always turn up.[19] Growth, he assures us, will resume – though, he warns, it could always be forestalled by the wrong sort of policies, so in fact it may not. Needless to say, Ridley has no more clue than the rest of us as to whether we will all finally revert to hunter-gathering. Instead, he simply confesses his faith in the spirit of innovation. In his Victorian reverence for the genius of inventors and entrepreneurs, he passes over the fact that innovation is simply one factor in a complex economic system, and by no means always the decisive one. As with most brands of naive progressivism, change, growth and innovation are viewed as inherently benign. Yet Hiroshima was a novelty, chemical weapons are a creative innovation, and methods of torture and surveillance have been progressively perfected. Samuel Johnson considered all change a great evil, which is not to say that he did not acknowledge its necessity.

Ridley declares himself mistrustful of markets in capital and assets as opposed to those in goods and services, while vigorously championing an economy to which the former are indispensable. Markets in assets, he concedes, 'are so automatically prone to bubbles and crashes that it is hard to design them so they work at all' (9), a damaging concession for a writer to whom market forces would seem as sacrosanct as organic carrots to Prince Charles. Ridley is a devout believer in the inherently beneficial workings of the market, while clamouring at the same time for its regulation. Insisting that he holds no brief for large corporations, he instantly proceeds to sing their praises. Walmart may crush trade unions and ruin small businesses, but its customers are thereby able to enjoy cheaper goods. In Ridley's Social Darwinist world, this would seem quite enough to render such practices acceptable. He concedes at one point that 'nuclear terrorism, rising sea levels and pandemic flu may yet make the twenty-first century a dreadful place', while assuring us in his penultimate sentence that 'the twenty-first century will be a magnificent time to be alive' (28 and 359). The contradiction can be resolved only by assuming that he regards being simultaneously drowned, blown to pieces, and infected with serious illness as an experience to be cherished.

Certain regions of the world, Ridley admits, may be convulsed by a descent into anarchy or authoritarianism, and a deep-seated enough economic depression may well trigger a large-scale war. Even so, 'so long as someone somewhere is incentivised to invent ways of serving others' needs better, then the rational optimist must conclude that the betterment of human lives will eventually resume' (32). But what if the war in question is of a global nuclear kind? And how long is 'eventually'? Konrad Lorenz ends his study *On Aggression* by claiming that the only hope for a non-violent humanity is some future genetic mutation that will turn us all into mutually affectionate creatures. It is not certain, however, that we can wait that long. How much transitional human misery is Ridley prepared to tolerate without ceasing to be dewy-eyed? And what if the innovations prove unprofitable? Capitalism, as the book conspicuously fails to point out, can impede inventive thought as well as promote it. The truth that the custodians of cheerfulness cannot stomach is that as long as there is contingency, there is the possibility of permanent failure. And, to be sure, the possibility of mind-shaking advances as well.

It is significant, incidentally, that Ridley fails to recognise the moral shabbiness of a social order in which individuals will be of service to others only if 'incentivised', presumably by a fat financial reward. He is baffled by the fact that anti-corporate activists have faith in 'leviathans' like the National Health Service while remaining 'suspicious of the behemoths that have to beg for your business' (111). It would not occur to a man for whom capitalism is as natural as moonlight that one might regard companies unmotivated by profit as morally superior to those that will stitch your wounds or teach arithmetic to your children only if you wave a credit card under their noses. Ridley describes capitalist corporations as 'temporary aggregations of people to help them do their producing in such a way as to help others do their consuming' (67), as though Microsoft and Coca-Cola were charitable institutions, to be ranked in their selfless devotion to human welfare with the Samaritans and the Boy Scouts. 'Helping others do their consuming' is a splendidly euphemistic way of portraying Exxon or Microsoft. It is as though one were to see the thief who makes off with your car as helping to reduce your waistline by forcing you to walk.

Despite his gung-ho flourishes, Ridley's buoyant vision is of a strangely muted kind. He admits, for example, that those who manned the mills and factories of early industrial England 'laboured for inhuman hours from an early age in conditions of terrible danger, noise and dirt, returning to crowded and insanitary homes through polluted streets, and had dreadful job security, diet, health care and education' (219). Nevertheless, he insists, they fared better than their farm-labourer ancestors. The conditions of an urban pauper of 1850 were atrocious, but the life of a rural pauper in 1700 was even worse. There's progress for you. A mere hundred million, Ridley claims, died of military conflict during the twentieth century, considerably fewer than those slain by warfare in hunter-gatherer societies. This is rather like claiming that a double amputee has a spectacular advantage over a quadruple one. Steven Pinker engages in a similar tactic in his *The Better Angels of Our Nature*, pointing out that the fifty-five million dead of the Second World War, viewed in proportion to the world population of the day, only just scrapes into the list of top ten catastrophes of all time. It is hard to imagine more heartwarming news. In similar spirit, Pinker drastically plays down the dangers of climate change, a topic that occupies, extraordinarily, no more than a page of his anodyne account. He even has the gall to remark that the shift from a fear of nuclear war, which he unaccountably imagines to have dwindled, to the prospect of 'damage to ecosystems, flooding, destructive storms, increased drought, and polar ice melt', represents 'a kind of progress'.[20]

'They killed, they enslaved, they extorted', Ridley remarks of early humanity, and this problem 'remained unsolved' for millennia (351). If this is to suggest that humankind has finally stumbled upon a solution to its own pugnacity, then Ridley ought surely to share this discovery with his readers. 'Violence', he remarks of this era, 'was a chronic and ever-present threat', as though such conflict were as much a thing of the past as the pterodactyl. In the earlier days of the species, we are told, 'some people got other people to do the work for them, and the result was pyramids and leisure for a few, drudgery and exhaustion for the many' (214). All of this, however, was to alter with the advance of technology, as though the practice of the few hiring the labour power of the many died out with the pharaohs. The truth is that the evolution of productive forces was by no means to provide leisure for the masses. On the contrary, for all their breathtaking technological progress, modern men and women work harder than their Neolithic ancestors. It is the social relations under which they labour – relations that the technologistic Ridley sets casually aside – which require them to do so.

There is another sense in which Ridley is far from the optimist he appears. His breeziness springs from a faith that the problems that have bedevilled humanity to date are en route to being resolved. But this is to concede that the human chronicle so far has indeed been dire. There would be no need for rousing the troops so robustly were this not so. And what has happened to date greatly outweighs in both substance and time-span the more recent advances that Ridley is keen to celebrate. Taken as a whole, then, the history of the species is by no means auspicious. It is true that we may find a cure for cancer, but this is scant comfort to the millions who have succumbed to its ravages in the past. The children of Africa may be plump-cheeked in some decades' time, but this cannot undo the fate of the millions who have already withered away. How long would a rosy future have to endure in order to redeem such a past? Could it ever do so? Even Christianity, which looks to a future state in which the tears of the afflicted will be wiped from their eyes and the bodies of the sick made whole, cannot blot disease and despair from the historical record. Not even God can unmake what has already occurred. Outside a Christian perspective, the dead are beyond hope. We cannot compensate them for the crimes of our ancestors. They are as far beyond our influence as the remote future. It is worth noting, incidentally, that Ridley's own observations on Christianity betray the theological illiteracy one has come to expect from secular liberals of his ilk. He imagines, for example, that Christians hold that the body is a mere container for the soul, a view that has about as much in common with the New Testament as Cornish nationalism.

If the past cannot simply be deleted, as Ridley would seem to advocate, it is not least because it is a vital constituent of the present. We can progress beyond it, to be sure, but only by means of the capabilities which it has bequeathed us. The habits bred by generations of supremacy and subservience, arrogance and inertia, are not to be unlearned overnight. Instead, they constitute an Ibsenesque legacy of guilt and debt which contaminates the roots of human creativity, infiltrating the bones and bloodstream of contemporary history and entwining itself with our more enlightened, emancipatory impulses. Ridley, by contrast, falls prey to a crudely progressivist distinction between a benighted past and a more luminous future. He fails to see not only how damagingly the past is interwoven with the present, but also how it can furnish us with precious resources for a more promising age to come. A civilisation that has only its contemporary experience to live by is poor indeed. If liberal modernisers like Ridley ought to be unnerved by the past, it is not only because so much of it threatens to undercut their bullishness. It is also because it contains legacies which might make for a transformation of the present far more deep-seated than they themselves would countenance.

Ridley is adamant that the one unchanging factor in history is human nature. Yet human nature, judging from the narrative to date, hardly provides grounds for exuberance. His conservatism is thus at odds with his progressivism. He is also inconsistent on the question, since alongside his belief in the immutability of human nature he touts a rather vulgar version of so-called commercial humanism, according to which the growth of commerce goes hand in hand with a general spread of civility. The more we trade, in short, the nicer we become. In the end, all Ridley can do is trust that one aspect of human nature – our ability to come up with smart new ideas – will outweigh our predilection for cruelty, self-interest, exploitation and the like. This seems an improbable wager.

Ridley believes in Progress, not just progress. In this sense, he is closer to Hegel and Herbert Spencer than he is to the average chief executive. A vision that was once thought to lie in ruins on the battlefields of the First World War has been revived in the early decades of the new millennium. *The Rational Optimist* unfurls a grand narrative that stretches from the origin of the species to a jubilant future, not just a modest set of reflections on the splendours of being alive in the twenty-first century. Humanity has evolved a collective intelligence which allows it to trade in ideas, and thereby to improve its condition. The fact that such collaboration has also given birth to torture and warfare passes discreetly unmentioned. Nor does the book grasp the point that collective intelligence, rather like Marx's faith in the unfolding of the productive forces, is far too general a conception to provide a yardstick of human development. Unabashed by the vagueness of the notion, Ridley speaks of progress as 'an inexorable tide in the affairs of men and women' (350). He is, in short, as much a full-blown determinist as the positivists and historicists of an age he believes we have put behind us.

In this respect, at least, he is a thoroughly retrograde avant-gardist. Progress would seem as irresistible as arthritis. We are as helpless before its unrolling as a badger before a bulldozer. When it comes to the individual, Ridley is a tamely conventional middle-class liberal who can apparently envisage no finer fulfilment than being allowed to make one's own choices about 'where to live, who to marry, how to express your sexuality and so on' (27). The mighty human narrative, unrolling across vast regions of space and countless tracts of time, comes down to the kind of thing they happen to favour in Hampstead and north Oxford. Yet the freedom he rates so highly at the personal level would seem to evaporate at the social one. The collective intelligence that drives human history remorselessly onward appears as resistant to challenge as the haughtiest despot. Similarly, there can be no flouting the hidden hand of the market, rather as there can be no spitting in the teeth of Providence.

Beneath his blitheness of spirit, then, Ridley is something of a fatalist. He writes, for example, that 'an income gap is an inevitable consequence of an expanding economy' (19). But why is this purveyor of future bliss such a prophet of doom? Can he not conceive of a form of social existence of which this would not be true? Why is he so stubbornly averse to conceptual innovation? What has become here of the creative imagination he claims to admire? Is it beyond our much-vaunted braininess to fashion a social system in which economic expansion would not spontaneously generate gross inequalities? Ridley's own imaginings are constrained by the immutable logic of the present. For him to be truly open to the indeterminacy of the future would be to saw away at the branch on which he is sitting. Instead, the future will simply be an improved version of the present – which is to say, no genuine future at all.

There are left-wing Pollyannas as well as liberal ones. In the closing pages of his *Literature and Revolution*, Leon Trotsky outlines his vision of the communist future:

> Man, who will learn to build people's palaces on the peaks of Mont Blanc and at the bottom of the Atlantic, will not only be able to add to his own life richness, brilliancy and intensity, but also a dynamic quality of the highest degree . . . He will make it his business to achieve beauty by giving the movement of his own limbs the utmost precision, purposefulness and economy in his work, his walk and his play. He will try to master first the semi-conscious and then the subconscious processes in his own organs, such as breathing, the circulation of the blood, digestion, reproduction, and, within necessary limits, he will try to subordinate them to the control of reason and will . . . Emancipated man will want to attain a greater equilibrium in the work of his organs and a more proportionate developing and wearing out of his tissues, in order to

reduce the fear of death to a rational reaction of the organism towards danger. . .

Man will make it his purpose to master his own feelings, to raise his instincts to the heights of consciousness, to make them transparent, to extend the wires of his will into hidden recesses, and thereby to raise himself to a new plane, to create a higher social biologic type, or, if you please, a superman . . . Man will become immeasurably stronger, wiser and subtler; his body will become more harmonic, his movements more rhythmic, his voice more musical. The forms of life will become dynamically dramatic. The average human being will rise to the heights of an Aristotle, a Goethe, or a Marx. And above this ridge new peaks will rise.[21]

It is not, perhaps, an entirely accurate portrait of Stalinist Russia. Soviet bank clerks failed to run for buses like ballet dancers, few shopkeepers learned how to control the circulation of their blood, while the voices that barked orders in the labour camps were not always melodious. The ever-sanguine Trotsky makes *The Rational Optimist* read like the Book of Job.

Hope is not always to be coupled with the doctrine of progress. In fact, Judeo-Christianity is one creed that breaks the link between them. There may indeed be progress in history from time to time, but it is not to be confused with redemption. It is not as though history as a whole is edging steadily closer to the Almighty, clambering from height to height until it glides into a glorious finale. For the New Testament, the *eschaton* or future kingdom of God is not to be mistaken for the consummation of history as a whole, and thus as the triumphal conclusion of a steadily upward trek, but as an event that breaks violently, unpredictably into the human narrative, upending its logic, defying its priorities, and unmasking its wisdom as foolishness. The Messiah does not sound the top note of the tune of history but breaks it abruptly off. Given that the most glaringly obvious fact about the Messiah is that he does not come, it falls to each generation to exercise a small portion of his power on behalf of the oppressed, bringing the poor to power in the hope of hastening his advent. In this sense, the Messiah's absence is not contingent but determinate: it clears a space in which the task of redeeming history is placed in the hands of humanity. If the revolutionary reversal promised by the Hebrew scriptures could be accomplished in our own time, filling the poor with good things and packing the rich off empty-handed, history would be brought abruptly to a close.

Yet the relation between history and the *eschaton* is not simply disjunctive. There is indeed a degree of continuity between them, but it is not in the manner of some stately teleology. In irrupting apocalyptically into historical time, the kingdom of God brings to fruition a pattern of transfigurative moments immanent within it, a fractured narrative of justice and comradeship which runs against the grain of what one might call its central plot. On this view, it is as though there is a coded pattern of hope woven into the fabric of history, a subtext whose letters are dispersed throughout its texture and will be assembled into a fully legible narrative only on Judgment Day. Only then, looking back on the course of secular history, will the secret compact between this and that strike for justice be visible, and all these events revealed as aspects of a single redemptive project.

It is to this subplot, or constellation of scattered yet affiliated moments, that Walter Benjamin in his *Theses on the Philosophy of History* gives the name of tradition. In his view, it is the task of the revolutionary historiographer to anticipate the backward glance of Judgment Day by forging affinities here and now between the *disjecta membra* of this secret history.[22] In doing so, he or she brings time to a momentary standstill, thus prefiguring its apocalyptic end. Messianic time, as Giorgio Agamben argues, is not some alternative dimension to common-or-garden *chronos* but the time such time takes to wrap itself up, a kind of inner dislocation or out-of-jointness in which it is contracted, consummated and recapitulated, caught between the already and the not-yet.[23] There is a relation between this vision and what Alain Badiou calls 'the rare and precious network of the ephemeral sequence of politics as truth'.[24]

If the task of the revolutionary historiographer is a pressing one, it is because the history that he or she seeks to redeem is in constant danger of perishing. It is the fate of the dispossessed to disappear. They are men and women who lack a lineage or succession, infertile creatures who thus require a different kind of memorial. They represent what Antoine Compagnon has called 'the history of that which has no descendants . . . the history of the failures in history'[25] – of those obscure strivings for justice which have melted and left no trace behind them in the annals of official history, thereby discrediting the whole notion of heritage, entitlement and lineal succession, but whose uncanny power the chronicler of the oppressed must seek to salvage. He or she must retrieve them from the oblivion that perpetually threatens to engulf them, storing them up for Judgment Day by blasting them free of the doomed narrative of which they form a part. We are here to make trouble on behalf of those who can no longer make trouble themselves, namely the dead.

To do so in Benjamin's view is to short-circuit time, cutting athwart its sterile evolution by placing a moment of historical emergency in direct relation to the coming of the Messiah. In this way, the memorialist can absolve the wretched of the earth, at least in memory, from the defeats that they endured in their time, bringing them to bear as a redemptive force on the political present. As Max Horkheimer writes, 'It is bitter to be misunderstood and to die in obscurity. It is to the honour of historical research that it projects light into that obscurity.'[26] He is thinking of historiography as the chronicle of the defeated, not as a saga recounted from the standpoint of Caesar. Among those who stand in need of remembrance is Benjamin himself. As a victim of fascism, he seems to have considered his own situation to be beyond redemption in the present. 'We ask of those who will come after us', he writes, 'not gratitude for our victories, but the remembrance of our defeats. This is a consolation – the only consolation, afforded to those who no longer have any hope of being consoled.'[27]

In Benjamin's eyes, there is indeed a universal history, but it does not constitute a grand narrative in the customary sense of the term. It is rather the persistent reality of suffering, which shares the universal form of a *grand récit* while lacking its teleological thrust. There is no meaning in such affliction, and therefore no point to history. Benjamin accordingly recasts Hegel and Marx's ultimately comic view of history in tragic, Messianic terms. If he can speak of history as a whole, it is because the state of emergency in which he penned his reflections on these matters, a moment of extreme danger shortly before his suicide while fleeing the Nazis, constituted a dialectical image in which history as such could be surreally condensed and foreshortened, viewed through the lens of his own personal and political crisis as a permanent state of emergency.

Even so, Benjamin sees the evanescent nature of history as an ironic source of hope, since this very fugitive quality points by negation to the advent of the Messiah. The decay of each instant of secular time is an index of the passing of history as such in relation to that momentous intervention. (For Christianity, one might add, the Messiah has already arrived – but in the guise of a tortured and executed political criminal, and thus in so obscenely unrecognisable a shape as to be effectively invisible.) What is most precious in Benjamin's eyes in the immense mound of wreckage known as history is that secret configuration of moments, standing out like a constellation of stars in a darkened sky, in which men and women throughout profane history have sought to hasten the arrival of the Messiah, striving to bring about the consummation of time by striking in their own age for the justice and fellowship he will eventually grant them. These moments are not to be seen as phases of some unbroken grand narrative; but neither do they exist simply as singularities, or as a series of glamorously existential *actes gratuits*. Instead, they are strategic moves in the coming of the kingdom. It is just that they do not deliver it as a freight train delivers its goods. The problem is how to look to the fruits of action without fetishising the future in the manner of bourgeois progressivism. Is there a way of acting strategically that would not fall foul of the instrumental rationality one seeks to resist?

What Benjamin is in pursuit of, then, is a nonprogressivist form of hope. His view of history takes issue alike with defeatism and triumphalism. It is strikingly close in some respects to the vision of Friedrich Nietzsche, who also believed in the need to create a future that might redeem the horror of the past – one that, rather like Benjamin's Angel of History, would break violently into the spurious stability of the present as an explosive 'here and now'. Nietzsche, however, is not out to compensate the dead for their sufferings at the hands of their exploiters, but to justify this whole wretched saga. If one can create an illustrious future, that of the *Übermensch*, the past can then be viewed retrospectively as an essential prologue to this achievement. The future for Nietzsche will be replete with triumph, whereas for Benjamin all historical times are empty when measured against the coming of the Messiah. Curiously, however, each of them can be regarded as full as well, since any one of them could constitute the strait gate through which the Saviour might enter. If every instant of time is simply void, it fails to be animated by an eager anticipation of the Messiah, the name of which is hope; yet if it is supercharged, crammed to bursting point, teeming with the burden of all previous moments in the manner of a certain historicism, it lacks the provisionality it needs to stand open to his arrival. Time is serialised, then, but not thereby emptied of value. There is a tension between anticipation and fulfilment, the vacancy of the present moment and the expectancy of it being plumped full to overflowing at any time.

For the ideology of progress, by contrast, all moments are devalued by the fact that each of them is no more than a stepping stone to a successor, the present a mere gangplank to the future. Every point of time is diminished in relation to an infinity of points still to come, as in Immanuel Kant's vision of unending progress. It was this prospect, one that strips human history of its catastrophic character, which Benjamin rejected as both morally complacent and politically quietist. It failed to see that it is not dreams of liberated grandchildren that spur men and women to revolt, but memories of oppressed ancestors. It is the past that furnishes us with the resources of hope, not just the speculative possibility of a rather more gratifying future. It is thus that Ernst Bloch, a friend of Benjamin, can speak of 'the still undischarged future in the past'.[28]

In fact, the past for Benjamin is curiously mutable. The progressivist regards previous history as dead and done with and the future as open and indeterminate. It is not, perhaps, entirely shapeless, since for the prophets of perfectibility it is constrained by a law of perpetual improvement. To that extent, the future is subject to at least one scientifically certain prediction – that it will represent an advance on the present. All the same, it seems self-evidently more open than the past. In Benjamin's view, however, the meaning of the past lies in the keeping of the present. Past history is fluid, labile, suspended, its sense yet to be fully determined. It is we who can endow it retrospectively with a definitive form, not simply by choosing to read it in a certain way but by virtue of our actions. It is up to us to determine whether, say, a child reared in twelfth-century Avignon belonged to a species whose destiny was to blow itself to bits. We must strive, then, to keep the past unfinished, refusing to accept its appearance of closure as the final word, springing it open once again by rewriting its apparent fatality under the sign of freedom.

Like a work of art, the meaning of the past evolves over time. Artworks for Benjamin resemble slow-burning fuses which generate fresh meanings as they enter upon new contexts, contexts that could not have been foreseen at the time of their production. Truths which have been secreted in these artifacts from the outset may be released for the first time by some conjuncture in their afterlife. Once more, the meaning of past events lies ultimately in the guardianship of the present. In a dialectical flash, a moment in the present finds an affinity with an instant of the past, and in granting that instant new meaning is also able to see itself afresh, as a potential fulfilment of that earlier promise. In some obscure sense, then, we are responsible for the past as well as for the present and future. The dead cannot be resurrected; but there is a tragic form of hope whereby they can be invested with new meaning, interpreted otherwise, woven into a narrative which they themselves could not have foretold, so that even the most inconspicuous of them will be, so to speak, mentioned in dispatches on the Last Day. Though there may be no actual continuity between them and ourselves, their struggles for emancipation can be incorporated into our own, so that whatever political gains we might manage to chalk up in our own time might help to vindicate their own baffled projects. By challenging the authority of our own rulers, Benjamin believes, we help to undermine the legitimacy of their predecessors as well, and in this sense strike a blow on behalf of those they mistreated. For Benjamin, astonishingly, even nostalgia can be lent an avant-garde inflection, rather as pathos and melancholy become weapons of class struggle in his hands. Rarely has sorrow been so strenuous an affair. Michael Lowy speaks of his 'deep, inconsolable sadness', a sadness that nonetheless turns his eyes to the future.[29] He is out to promote a revolutionary version of an unstaunchable homesickness for the past – one in which, as in Proust's great novel, past events are brought to fruition under the retroactive gaze of the present, and as such appear more charged with meaning than they did the first time round. *Einmal ist keinmal,* observes the novelist Milan Kundera. For Benjamin, events without an afterlife have an air of ontological fragility about them and, without such rituals of remembrance as radical historiography, are always in danger of sinking without trace into the political unconscious.

Messianic time is thus at odds with the doctrine of progress. Indeed, it sees no hope in secular history as such. Left to its own devices, that history will simply generate new wars, catastrophes and theatres of barbarism. Benjamin, in short, is too quick to identify a belief in the historical immanence of hope with fatalism and triumphalism. A more orthodox theology than his would hold that there are certain in built human capacities for hope, but that this is no guarantee that love and justice will flourish on this side of the Parousia. For Benjamin's Angel of History, by contrast, the point is to have done with history altogether. Turning his horror-struck countenance to the mounting rubbish heap of the past, he strives to arrest time so as to awaken the dead and bring about eternity here and now. By pulling the emergency brake on history in a 'cessation of happening', he aims to clear a space into which the Messiah might enter. What thwarts his attempts is the ideology of progress, which in mistaking the infinite for the eternal imagines that redemption lies at the end of history rather than at the heart of it. It also assumes that profane history can deliver under its own steam the justice of which humanity stands in need. In Benjamin's view, the Kantian prospect of infinite progress is an image of hell, involving as it does the eternal repetition of the commodity form. It is this specious doctrine which blows the Angel relentlessly backward into the future, unable to stem the flow of time for long enough to bring off his audacious rescue. The myth of progress is also the lie that the catastrophe of the past, to which the Angel's appalled gaze is turned, is an essential prelude to a finer future. The Angel knows any such theodicy to be an illusion, which is why he strives to break open paradise here and now in disregard of all such teleology. If there is indeed such a thing as eternity, it must lie at the core of time, not at its conclusion. Yet the Angel is unable to resist the force of this formidable ideological fiction, which is why the dead remain unawakened and the long catastrophe of history continues to roll forward.

Marxism is rather less ambiguous about the idea of progress than Judeo-Christianity. Marx himself seems to have believed for the most part in a steady evolution of the productive forces; but this by no means entails a cumulative increase in human well-being, as it does, by and large, for the mechanistically-minded Ridley. On the contrary, as we have seen already, the flourishing of human power and prosperity also involves the breeding of poverty, inequality and exploitation. In the end, Marx considers, all men and women will be able to share in the spiritual and material wealth that the future will inherit from the past. To that extent, the human narrative has a comic outcome. Yet the mechanisms by which this wealth is amassed are those of class society, and thus the tale of one form of exploitation after another. It is this that Marx has in mind when he claims that history progresses by its bad side. Viewed from one angle, history represents a movement onward and upward, as human beings acquire more complex needs and desires and evolve new powers and capabilities, all on the back of their material development. Seen from another angle, however, it is a question of lurching from one form of organised injustice to another, so that the story is also a tragic one. Tragedy does not necessarily involve a sticky end; it may simply mean that one has to be hauled through hell in order to achieve a modicum of well-being. And this would certainly seem to be the case for Marxism.

There is a serious problem with this case, quite apart from Marx's occasionally overlooking the fact that the productive forces may stagnate for long stretches of time. Is the theory a kind of theodicy, or justification of evil? Is Marx claiming that injustice now is a necessary condition of justice later? Socialism, he believes, is possible only on the basis of a previous expansion of the productive forces. Otherwise one will end up with what he scathingly calls 'generalised scarcity', as history was to witness in the Soviet Union and its satellites. Yet what expands the productive forces most effectively is capitalism, and capitalism in Marx's eyes is a question of injustice. This, then, is why he insists that 'the development of the capacities of the *human species* takes place at the cost of the majority of individuals and even classes'.[30] Good in the long run would seem to involve adversity in the short term. The affluence that will eventually facilitate the realm of freedom is itself the fruit of unfreedom. And this sounds disturbingly like a full-blown theodicy, even if there are some vital caveats to be inserted. For one thing, there is a difference between doing evil in the hope that good may eventually come of it, and seeking to turn an existing evil to one's own advantage. For another thing, there is no suggestion in Marx's writing that the advent of socialism will retrospectively justify the crimes of class society.

Even if there are those who are fortunate to disembark at the destination of a just society, there remains the question of those who died in the tunnels and perished on the sidings – those who were not delivered by the engine of history to a felicitous terminus, but whose very names were expunged from the historical record, and who lived lives of such fruitless, back-breaking toil that it might truly be asked in Schopenhauerian spirit whether they would not have been better off never being born. What of the countless millions who have fallen by the wayside, unfulfilled and unremembered? The 'most urgent question of socialist construction', writes Fredric Jameson, 'remains that of individual sacrifice, and of the renunciations made by present generations for the benefit of generations in a future they will not themselves see'.[31] 'What has happened to the human beings who have fallen', comments Max Horkheimer, 'no future can repair . . . Amid this immense indifference, human consciousness alone can become the site where the injustice suffered can be abolished, the only agency that does not give in to it.'[32] The reclamation of the dead in memory, however, seems a poor substitute for some more palpable act of restitution. What, too, of those obscure, innumerable tragedies which no purely political solution could ever repair? It is striking how few Marxists appear to have asked themselves whether even the most resplendently emancipated future could outweigh this saga of sorrow. And this is one sense in which Marx's theory, despite himself, can properly be called tragic.

Not all commentators agree. George Steiner, for whom any vigorous faith in humanity spells the ruin of tragedy, argues in *The Death of Tragedy* that neither Marxism nor Christianity can be classed as a tragic creed. 'The least touch of any theology that has a compensating Heaven to offer the tragic hero is fatal', he insists.[33] He is thinking, however, of these doctrines' affirmative visions of the future, not of the alarmingly steep price one has to pay for them. Resurrection does not cancel the reality of crucifixion, or communism the horrors of class society. Indeed, one might claim that part of what disappears when the Christian doctrine of hope becomes the secular ideology of progress is precisely its tragic dimension. Like Steiner, Avery Dulles maintains that Christianity puts paid to tragedy. 'The Christian', he writes, 'has no need to shrink in fear from the prospect of poverty, disgrace, captivity, physical pain, apparent failure, even death. None of these eventualities dejects him because he has been taught that to share in Christ's sufferings is the normal way to prepare oneself to share in his glory.'[34] Dulles seems to have forgotten that Jesus himself is portrayed as shrinking from pain, failure, captivity, disgrace and death in Gethsemane. If he is to be an authentic martyr, the Gospel-writers must demonstrate that he does not wish to die. The martyr yields up a life he regards as precious, not one he rates as worthless. There is no merit in embracing a suffering you regard as a mere springboard to celestial bliss. Those who do not shrink from pain or disgrace are obtuse rather than admirable, whatever Dulles may piously avow. Besides, since the New Testament seems to suggest that the coming of God's kingdom will be heralded by apocalyptic turmoil, its hope is not easily distinguishable from fear and trembling. It is a curious feature of Christianity that this spectacular crack-up belongs to a narrative which is fundamentally comic.

We have seen that for Christian faith, the future kingdom is immanent in human history yet at the same time discontinuous with it. If it is stealthily at work in the present like yeast in a lump of dough, it also steals upon men and women like a thief in the night. To put the matter differently: grace builds upon a human nature which is inherently receptive to it, but transfigures it in the act of doing so. It follows that faith in humanity is a question of realism, but so, too, is a sober estimate of whatever in it needs to be repaired. There is hope, then, but no callow optimism. Translated into political terms, pure immanentism is bound up with the kind of leftist historicism against which Benjamin set his face. On this theory, there is a dynamic at work in history which will bring it in the fullness of time to socialist fruition. Sheer apocalypticism, by contrast, is equally implausible. On this view, the transformative event erupts unpredictably into a degenerate history in which there is little to be valued, and can find no grounding there. If it redeems the present, it is not rooted in it. It is a radical Protestant perspective, the political correlative of which can be found in our own day in the work of Alain Badiou. For this style of thought, the revolutionary event must indeed be miraculous, since there would seem little in a fallen world to warrant it. If historicism invests too much trust in the works of time, apocalypticism reveals too little.

For a more orthodox current of Marxism, as for the Catholic lineage of Christianity, a valid future must be dimly discernible in the present. For Marxism, it can be found in those forces which are bred by the current system yet which are capable of unlocking its contradictions. For there to be genuine hope, the future must be anchored in the present. It cannot simply irrupt into it from some metaphysical outer space. At the same time, the yeast-like powers at work in the present do so in a way that finally surpasses its limits, pointing to a condition beyond our current imaginings. A future that could be adequately captured in the language of the present would be too complicit with the status quo, and so would scarcely count as a genuine future at all.

Whatever one may make of hope, then, it is certainly not a question of optimism. Yet there is, in fact, surprisingly little philosophical reflection on what hope consists in. It is to this question that we can now turn.

2

What is Hope?

THE THREE SO-CALLED theological virtues of faith, hope and charity all have their corrupt corollaries. Faith is likely to lapse into credulity, charity into sentimentalism, and hope into self-delusion. Indeed, it is hard to pronounce the word 'hope' without evoking the prospect of it being dashed, as adjectives such as 'faint' or 'forlorn' leap spontaneously to mind. There seems something incorrigibly naive about the very notion, whereas there appears to be a certain maturity about moroseness. Hope suggests a tremulous, half-fearful expectation, the mere ghost of a robust assurance. In modern times, it has had almost as bad a press as nostalgia, which is more or less its opposite. Hope is a slender reed, a castle in the air, agreeable company but a poor guide, fine sauce but scanty food. If April is the cruellest month for *The Waste Land*, it is because it breeds false hopes of regeneration.

There are even those for whom hope is a kind of indignity, fit for social reformers rather than tragic heroes. George Steiner admires a form of 'absolute tragedy' that would be 'uncontaminated' by anything as despicably petty-bourgeois as hope. 'In high tragedy', he remarks, 'nullity devours like a black hole',[1] a condition that the slightest whiff of hope could only adulterate. The grandeur of tragedy, Steiner protests, is diminished by such futile hankerings. This is not, as it happens, true of Aeschylus's *Oresteia*, or indeed of Shakespeare's tragic drama, both of which should be high enough for anyone's taste. But tragedy, so Steiner holds, is not natural to Shakespeare, which is why he insists on diluting the pure essence of despair with various vulgar hints of redemption. The vision of Christopher Marlowe's *Doctor Faustus*, by contrast, an egregiously uneven, broken-backed play, is unremittingly cold-eyed, and thus 'profoundly non-Shakespearean'. The adjective is intended as complimentary. Tragedy spurns all social hope, and is thus an inherently anti-leftist mode. Pessimism is a political standpoint.[2] The Catholic philosopher Peter Geach takes an equally bleak-eyed view of hope, if for rather different reasons. If hope is not grounded in the Christian gospel, he insists, there is no hope at all.[3] It is hard to believe that one's eager expectation of a square meal is rendered null and void by the fact that it is not grounded in the death and resurrection of Jesus. Even if Christianity is the only final hope for humanity, it does not follow that any aspiration which falls short of the kingdom of God is doomed to failure.

The political left can be as wary of hope as the Steinerian right. Claire Colebrook, for example, toys with the idea of a 'hopeless feminism'. 'Feminism, it seems,' she writes, 'may need to abandon hope – hope for a richer boyfriend, a larger pair of breasts, a slimmer pair of thighs and an even more unattainable handbag of the day – in order to imagine a future that would release "us" from the clichés on which we have glutted and which have drugged us into a lack of nerve. Utopia could only be achieved through an intense hopelessness.'[4] It is not a politics Colebrook unreservedly endorses, and for good reason: if women may have a number of false or negative hopes, they have a range of authentic ones as well. Even so, the Left's suspicion of hope is not entirely groundless. Images of utopia are always in danger of confiscating the energies that might otherwise be invested in its construction.

Those who have hope are likely to appear less tough-minded than those who lack it, even though there are times when nothing is more extravagantly unrealistic than pessimism. In the era of modernity, gloom appears a more sophisticated stance than cheerfulness. Hope in the wake of Buchenwald and Hiroshima seems no more than an unfounded faith that the future will represent an advance on the present, recalling Samuel Johnson's sardonic description of remarriage as the triumph of hope over experience. Yet even the most terrible events of our epoch can yield grounds for hope. As Raymond Williams points out, if there were those who perished in the Nazi camps, there were also those who gave their lives to rid the world of those who built them.[5]

By and large, hope has been the poor relation of the theological virtues, inspiring fewer scholarly explorations than faith and love. Despite its title, Peter Geach's book *Truth and Hope* has nothing whatsoever to say about hope, and his discussion of it in *The Virtues* is notably thinner than his comments about faith. It is worth noting that the three dispositions are closely interrelated. St Augustine writes in the *Enchiridion* that 'there is no love without hope, no hope without love, and neither hope nor love without faith'.[6] Faith is a kind of loving commitment or passionate conviction, one that for orthodox Christian doctrine is made possible in the first place by God's besottedness with humanity. 'A believer is someone who is in love', writes Kierkegaard in *The Sickness Unto Death*. Faith is a question of trust, which in turn involves a form of charity or self-giving. It is a steadfast conviction that the other will not let you slip through his fingers, and to trust that one will not be abandoned is the foundation of hope. In fact, the *Oxford English Dictionary* gives 'a feeling of trust' as an archaic meaning of 'hope'. Hope is a confidence that one's project will prevail, what one commentator calls an 'active commitment to the desirability and realisability of a certain end'.[7] As such, it involves desire and thus, in a broad sense of the term, love. It is faith that reveals what one may legitimately hope for, and both virtues are ultimately rooted in charity.

Love for Thomas Aquinas differs from hope in being already united with its object, at least in spirit; yet as Denys Turner comments, paraphrasing Aquinas, 'true charity generates the sort of hope that causes one friend to count on another, for it is on those who through charity are our friends that we can most perfectly rely'.[8] In Aquinas's view, faith and charity are logically prior to hope, whereas for both Kant and John Stuart Mill it is hope in

God which leads us to postulate his existence. The same is true of Miguel de Unamuno, who claims in *The Tragic Sense of Life* that we believe because we hope, not vice versa. Former US President Bill Clinton once yoked the virtues of faith and hope together by declaring, 'I still believe in a place called Hope', a reference to the town where he grew up. If he had modified his sentiment to 'I still believe in a place I love called Hope', he could have neatly combined the three theological virtues.

In general, the more rational one's grounds for faith, the more one may hope, since the more probable it is that one's faith will be vindicated. To have faith in the human passion for justice, for example, to which the whole of history bears witness, is to have a reasonable hope that it will not vanish from the earth without a struggle, even if it does not finally prevail. For Christianity, to have faith in the God who raised Jesus from the dead is to have grounds for hope that humanity itself will ultimately undergo such a transformation. All the same, one can have faith in human capabilities while rating their chances of success as fairly negligible, so that hope does not always follow on the heels of faith. Conversely, you might hope for peace and justice with only a meagre faith in the power of humanity to deliver them. Or you might feel an impassioned love for humankind without having the slightest faith in it as a species, or the faintest hope that its condition might signally improve. A despairing love is by no means out of the question.

What, however, if hope were an illusion? It would be no obvious reason to write it off. For Alexander Pope's *Essay on Man*, hope is a therapeutic fiction, one that sustains us in existence by persuading us to pursue one chimerical goal after another:

> Hope springs eternal in the human breast;
> Man never is, but always to be blest.

It is a deceptive statement, considerably less positive than the brisk heroic couplet form makes it sound. The word 'eternal' invests the idea of hope with a touch of divine glory, though it actually means something like 'perpetual'. What is enduring about us is our dissatisfaction. 'Man never is, but always to be blest' sounds suitably pious but is in fact sardonic. We persist in hoping because we are constantly disenchanted, a persistence that one can regard either as a plucky refusal of defeat or an obtuse indifference to the lessons of experience. There is certainly an implication that hope springs eternal because it is blind to its own emptiness, an obduracy that contrasts with the suave intelligence of the lines themselves. For Pope and Samuel Johnson, as for some of the major thinkers of late modernity (Schopenhauer, Nietzsche, Freud), consciousness is always laced with an admixture of false consciousness, and would be unable to function without it. Hope is an Apollonian mirage or Ibsenite life-lie by which futility is kept at bay while the gods laugh cynically up their sleeves. There may be no hope; but unless we act as though there is, that possibility is likely to become a certainty. The Freud of *The Future of an Illusion* views religious hope as a nurse recounting fairy tales to a child, and wishes to purge the world of such consoling fictions. Erik Erikson regards hope, which first manifests itself in the infant's trust in its parents, as 'both the earliest and the most indispensable virtue in being alive'; yet he also writes that in the course of the small child's development, 'concrete hopes will, at a time when a hoped-for event or state comes to pass, prove to have been quietly superseded by a more advanced set of hopes',[9] a periphrastic way of suggesting that as soon as we get what we want, we want something else.

Nor is such scepticism confined to modernity. In general, the ancient Greeks viewed hope more as bane than boon. Euripides calls it a curse on humanity. Plato warns us in the *Timaeus* that hope can lead us astray. Thomas Aquinas acidly remarks that hope abounds in youth, drunks and the kind of fools who lack deliberation.[10] 'So we never live', comments Pascal in his *Pensées*, 'but we hope to live.' Byron calls hope a hollow-cheeked harlot. Kierkegaard describes hope in *Repetition* as a charming maid that slips through one's fingers, though it is secular rather than religious aspirations he has in mind. Jean-Paul Sartre speaks of *le sale espoir*. For a good many thinkers down the centuries, delusion is the dynamic of human existence, and whether this is to be affirmed or lamented depends on whether one lays stress on the striving or the self-deceit. Amnesiac creatures that we are, we suppress the vacuity of our past hopes in order to chase yet another alluring will-o'-the-wisp, and this endless manufacture of self-oblivion is known as human existence.

Seen in this light, hope is a fetishism of the future, one that reduces the past to so much prologue and the present to mere empty expectancy. There are accordingly times when it does not sound all that different from despair. If it is the most pestilent of the evils to emerge from Pandora's box, it is because it stops us putting an end to ourselves, and thus from putting an end to all the other evils that beset us. The legend of Pandora is interestingly ambiguous on the question of whether hope is sickness or cure, or, in some homeopathic fashion, both at the same time. Is hoping for a therapy for our woes actually part of them, since it prevents us from cheating them by suicide? Does hope, like Schopenhauer's malevolent Will, keep us alive so that we may be further tormented, like a torturer emptying a bucket of water over his victim's head?

On this view, hope is the crack in the present through which a future can be glimpsed, but it is also what hollows the human subject into nonbeing. It devaluates each moment, laying it on the sacrificial altar of a future fulfilment that will never arrive. Without this constant process of being pitched ahead of oneself, grabbing for a contentment that melts in one's grasp, there would be no specifically human life. 'We're not happy and we can't be happy', remarks Vershinin in Chekhov's *Three Sisters*; 'we only want happiness.' Hope, like desire as such, is the way in which the human animal is nonidentical with itself, its existence an eternal not-yet, its substance a kind of suspension. It represents what Karl Rahner calls 'a basic modality of human existence', not simply a mental attitude.[11]

For Samuel Johnson, this state of non-self-identity is good reason for dejection. Yet Johnson's attitude to hope is interestingly ambiguous, since he also regards it as an indispensable goad to human endeavour. In his verse 'On the Death of Dr Robert Levet', it is bluntly described as 'delusive'; yet Johnson also comments in the *Rambler* that 'it is necessary to hope, though hope should always be deluded; for hope itself is happiness, and its frustrations, however frequent, are less dreadful than its extinction'.[12] Delusion or fruitful falsehood is at least preferable to despair. In Aeschylus's *Prometheus Bound*, Prometheus tells the Chorus that among his other benefactions to humankind has been the gift of 'blind hopefulness', to which they reply, unironically, 'Your gift brought them great blessing.' Perhaps the only happiness we can attain is a hope that it will arrive.

For all his scepticism, Johnson can describe hope as 'the chief blessing of man',[13] though he adds that only that hope is rational which we are certain will not deceive us. He may well have considered that there was only one member of such a class (the Christian hope for salvation), in which case it is easy to see how he could rate the virtue so highly while at the same time regarding it (as in his novel *Rasselas*) as mostly spurious. It was the difference between sacred and secular aspirations that counted. Perhaps hope for Johnson involves a kind of cognitive dissonance or redemptive irony, as one affirms and disbelieves in the same breath. It may be that optimism of the will counteracts pessimism of the intellect. As a modern philosopher tortuously puts it, 'Someone who is *hopeful* that *p* typically acts as if he "assumes the best" – again, that it *is* so. And yet he needn't believe it so, or even probably so; he might even think it probably *not* so.'[14] We shall see later, however, that though hope need not involve the probable, it does indeed hinge on the possible.

The achievement of F. Scott Fitzgerald's *The Great Gatsby* lies among other things in the fact that the novel does not allow us to adopt an unambiguous attitude to the grandiose dreams of its protagonist. Gatsby turns out to be a crook and a corrupt fantasist, but there is a splendour all the same about his implacable desire for Daisy, a truth secreted at the heart of its falsehood. Gatsby has what the narrator calls 'a heightened sensitivity to the promises of life . . . an extraordinary gift for hope, a romantic readiness such I have never found in any other person and which it is not likely I shall ever find again'. His hopes, to be sure, will come to nothing, since the force of the past proves stronger than the pull of the future:

> Gatsby believed in the green light, the orgastic [*sic*] future that year by year recedes before us. It eluded us then, but that's no matter – tomorrow we will run faster, stretch out our arms farther . . . And one fine morning –
>
> So we beat on, boats against the current, borne back ceaselessly into the past.

The past exists no more than the future; yet it has the edge over the latter in having once loomed large, which is why it can still wield an authority denied to what is yet to come. If the present cannot escape the orbit of the past, it is not only because the past is for the most part what we are made of, but because, as with Gatsby's forlorn impulse to repeat, it has no desire to do so. Much of the present consists of an effort to recapture what has been irreparably lost. It is as though it is little more than an opportunity for the past to happen again, this time as comedy. The world itself, writes the satirist Karl Kraus, is simply an erroneous, deviating, circuitous way back to paradise.

Even so, the fact that Gatsby is so poignantly self-deceived is not allowed entirely to tarnish his aura or dispel his enigma, rather as the vision of those refugees from Europe who first set foot in America has not been entirely undermined by the nation's chequered later history. In what *The Great Gatsby* parochially and presumptuously calls 'that last and greatest of all human dreams', 'for a transitory moment man must have held his breath in the presence of this continent, compelled into an aesthetic contemplation he neither understood nor desired, face to face for the last time in history with something commensurate to his capacity to wonder'. In similar vein, the narrator of Paul Auster's *City of Glass* imagines the entry of these pioneers into the New World as 'the quickening impulse of utopian thought, the spark that gave hope to the perfectibility of human life', even though we are aware that the results of this colonial adventure were by no means unequivocally positive.

On this rather questionable view, there is a utopian core even to the most baneful or megalomaniac of hopes, as we shall see later in the work of Ernst Bloch. It is thus that Fitzgerald's novel can admire 'the colossal vitality of [Gatsby's] illusion', even though its consequences are death and destruction. Properly deciphered, so the story runs, every death-dealing hope can yield us a dim, distorted echo of a life-yielding one, rather as the most calamitous of human actions represents a bungled attempt at happiness. In this sense, the inauthentic can serve as the medium of the authentic. There is, perhaps, a specifically American literary motif at work here. In *Moby-Dick*, Ahab achieves tragic stature by the very tenacity with which he remains true to a lethal delusion, and the same might be said in less epic mode of Arthur Miller's Willy Loman. In formalistic style, one is invited to admire the passion and steadfastness of a commitment regardless of its disastrously wrongheaded content.

Is there a difference between hope and desire? There are times when the distinction would appear fairly minimal. 'I hope so' can simply mean 'I wish so'. There is no metaphysical abyss between wanting a cigar and hoping for one. The philosopher Gabriel Marcel sees hope as a form of love and desire as covetous and egocentric,[15] but this overlooks the fact that there can be malignant hopes and benign desires. Both hope and desire may be moral states, but neither is necessarily so: you can hope that it won't snow or desire a pickled egg. Desire is often for a specific object, whereas hope's goal is generally a state of affairs; yet you can desire that a state of affairs come about, or hope for a smoother complexion. One can also speak of hoping *in* someone (which is different from having hope *for* them), meaning that you have faith that they will not fail you in delivering what you want. There is a sense in which you can desire (and certainly love) what you already have, but you cannot hope for what you already have.[16] Hope and desire may be mutually at odds: you may want a cigarette but hope not to succumb to your craving. Or you may hope for something consciously while harbouring an unconscious aversion to it. Hope and faith may also be discrepant: you may hope to die of rabies, for example, though without any belief that you will. You can feel strenuous hope even when the evidence is weak, but not firm conviction. To believe that something will happen is to expect it to, but to hope that it will is not necessarily to do so.[17]

'I hope to be in New York next October' registers an expectation that you will be, whereas 'I wish I were Mick Jagger' does not. 'I hope for release from this torment' expresses a wish but also perhaps an expectation. Precisely because it anticipates rather than simply desires, hope must intend the possible, or at least what those in the grip of it regard as possible, which is not necessarily true of desire.[18] Those who hope to become president of the World Bank are more likely to be granted this dubious honour than those who simply dream of being, since the fact that they hope for the post implies that it is possible to obtain it. Thomas Hobbes speaks of hope in *Leviathan* as 'an appetite with an opinion of attaining', while Paul Ricoeur famously describes it as 'a passion for the possible'.[19] Stan van Hooft points out that one can speak of a situation as hopeless but not as wishless, since one can wish for what one knows to be unattainable.[20] One can always desire, but one cannot always hope. You may want to be a stoat or a citizen of Periclean Athens, but you cannot hope to be either. Someone may wish that she had never been born, but she cannot hope for it.

There is nothing necessarily foolish about hoping in vain, but it is foolish to hope unreasonably. Gabriel Marcel maintains that one can hope for anything short of the impossible, so that a hope is not invalidated by the gross improbability of it ever coming to pass. It is irrational to hope for the impossible, but not for the vastly improbable. Hope requires fewer grounds than belief: it may be rational to hope that something will come about, but

irrational to believe that it will. One can, to be sure, hope unreasonably, in the sense that you can continue to expect the outcome
you desire even when it is blatantly unrealistic to do so; but to
believe unreasonably that one's hopes may be fulfilled is to believe mistakenly that they are feasible. One can also desire unreasonably. For psychoanalytic theory, those who desire unreasonably risk falling ill of neurosis. Unreasonable hopes may include
too timorous ones. The prejudice that hope is naive forgets that
there are situations in which vigorous hope is wholly appropriate
and faint ones unrealistic. This is scarcely the case with the wars
and genocides of the twentieth century; yet one might question
even so whether a portraitist of the period as superb as W. G. Se-
bald is entirely realistic in his unremitting cheerlessness.

Impossibility cancels hope but not desire: you may long to
inveigle the current dictator of North Korea into a gay nightclub
in downtown Denver, while recognising that your wish is futile.
Abraham appears to hope for the impossible when he desires that
his son might be saved from the knife he is commanded to wield
against him, but because all things are possible with Yahweh, his
hope is not in fact vain. It is also worth noting that I can hope for
what is possible for you (to become the proud mother of triplets,
for example) but not for me. Though death marks the end of
hoping for ourselves, one's hope for others may stretch beyond
the grave. This does not mean that such hopes are always selfless.
I might hope that you will continue my lifelong vendetta against
rival Elvis Presley impersonators when I myself am no longer
around to do so.

Robert Audi points out that to have faith that something will
come about is not usually to be surprised when it does, whereas
someone who simply hopes for it may well be.[21] He also claims
that you can be ashamed of hoping that something will happen but not of having faith that it will, though having faith that
your stealthy schemes for world dominion will pass undetected
is surely sufficient cause for shame.[22] A realised hope regularly
modifies expectation. As with desire, the object of hope may
arrive in transfigured guise, or one's hope may have altered or

lapsed altogether by the time it appears. For Freud, desire tends to miss its mark, sent awry by the deeper process of longing (the unconscious) with which it is entangled. It may also be that one only really discovers the true nature of one's hope when it is actually realised. Perhaps Jesus's comrades were hoping for his resurrection but did not know that they were until it took place.

Thomas Aquinas remarks that 'a man does not hope for what lies wholly beyond his own capacities',[23] adding the rider that hope must be arduous in the sense that its object must be hard to attain. Hope for Aquinas is 'a movement or stretch of appetite towards some difficult good'.[24] You cannot hope for the impossible, but neither in Aquinas's view is the virtue best exemplified by the ready-to-hand and easy-to-achieve. Its object, he writes, is a good that lies in the future and that is difficult but possible to attain.[25] To this extent, hope is the enemy of idle utopianism as well as of despair. Yet hope is not always a question of our own efforts, arduous or otherwise. One may hope for what lies in principle beyond one's capacities, which is not the same as hoping for the impossible. You may hope that it doesn't rain, for example, or that your current mild, socially functional paranoia will not blossom into full-blown psychosis.

Pace Aquinas, it is not clear why one should not use the word 'hope' of some fairly trifling desire-plus-expectation, such as hoping that one's trousers will stay up for the duration of the degree ceremony. To say 'I hope to see you tomorrow' does not usually imply that the encounter is likely to prove an exacting affair, involving a series of obstacles to be heroically surmounted. Besides, there is a form of hope that does not really view its own fulfilment as feasible. 'Next year in the New Jerusalem!' would be an example. Most of those who chant such a slogan are unlikely to believe that heaven or communism will actually come to pass in a year's time, even though history can change with lightning speed; but the words have a performative force even so, lending heart to those who pronounce them, and perhaps in doing so making the advent of a desirable future fractionally closer. To hope that communism will hold sway across the globe by next July is a rhetorical way of articulating a hope that one does indeed regard as reasonable. In this sense, the hyperbolic shell of the proposition conceals a rational kernel.

Hope is one species of what Aristotle calls rational desire, as opposed to the kind of desire that, like wanting to eat or sleep, is simply a matter of appetite. To hope for the overthrow of the monarchy, for example, is not just to desire it but to believe that it is attainable, to acknowledge it as a good, to trust that it will come about, to look forward to its arrival with a sense of expectancy and perhaps also with a degree of confidence, and so on, all of which involves reason. For Immanuel Kant, hope is rationally justified only in the case of a virtuous individual, who alone has a reasonable expectation of the happiness everyone desires.[26] For the most part, both hope and desire look to the future, orientated as they are to attainments which are currently nonexistent. I say that hope looks to the future 'for the most part' because it is possible to hope that one's daughter has not gone to pieces in the driving test she is currently taking, or that one did not disgrace oneself at last night's party by climbing yet again into one's badger costume. It is a point lost on almost all theorists of the subject (including, as we have just seen, Aquinas), who view the virtue only in terms of futurity. You can, needless to say, be future-directed in supremely trivial ways. Those with trust in the future, write two particularly perceptive observers of humanity, 'make "to do" lists, use day planners, and wear wrist watches; they also balance their check books – all these activities imply an orientation to the future'.[27] We have come a long way from St Augustine. When it comes to future-oriented hope, we may note that its object may already be in existence even if the state of attaining it is not. St Paul remarks in his Epistle to the Romans that nobody hopes for what is before his eyes, but not all hopes are to be modelled on eschatological ones. You can hope to demolish the very pork pie you are eyeing with such cupidity, though it is true that the act of demolishing it is still to come. Hope and desire are also alike in the fact that both expire in the act of fulfilment. In consummating a wish, one simultaneously annuls it.

Because hope involves a degree of expectation, it is generally speaking more narrationally inflected than desire, which may
simply shuttle from one object to the next with no very obvious
storyline. By contrast there is the ghost of a plot to hope, which
links a present impulse to a future fulfilment. There is a similar
plotting about the act of promising. To hope means to project
oneself imaginatively into a future that is grasped as possible, and
thus as in some shadowy sense already present, rather than simply to languish in the grip of an appetite. It is true that the future
does not exist, any more than does the past; but rather as the past
lives on in its effects, so the future may be present as a potential.
It is what Ernst Bloch terms the 'Not-yet-conscious', meaning
the way that the future can be found incubating within both the
past and present in the form of a dim premonition of what is
to come, and thus as a kind of inverted reminiscence.[28] These
premonitions in Bloch's view take the form not of mental acts
but of material phenomena: artworks, cityscapes, political events,
popular customs, religious rituals and so on. We cannot know the
future directly, but for Bloch we can feel its ghostly pull all the
same, like a force that warps space out of true. It is to be found in
the unfinished nature of the actual, discernible as a hollow at its
heart. Potentiality is what articulates the present with the future,
and thus lays down the material infrastructure of hope. Indeed,
it is because there is strictly speaking no present – because every
present is radically in excess of itself, apprehended in the act of
retaining a trace of the past while passing instantaneously over
into a future – that hope is conceivable. But also, of course, fearful anticipation and doleful expectancy.

Hope, then, is a more positive disposition than desire. The
latter tends to revolve around a sense of lack, while the former
mixes this disquiet with a degree of tensed expectancy. Hope for
Aquinas has something of the discomfort of desire because its
object is not yet secured, but counterpoints this restiveness with
an eager reaching out to that end. It is a movement toward the
good, not simply a craving for it. Hope originates in desire, but
adds to it a certain buoyancy or touch of elation, which is not

the case with common-or-garden craving. There is a felt link between a felicity still to come and one's current situation; and this lends hope a teleological thrust less obvious in the case of desire, at least in the psychoanalytic sense of the term, which in the end knows no more gratifying fulfilment than to loop back upon itself. It is true, however, that there are also faint or wan hopes, where the link between present and future is weak, since the chances of attaining one's object are remote.

Both hope and desire involve an interplay of presence and absence, as a future is brought dimly into focus in the very act of longing for it. The same can be true of imagination. A robust hope, however, does not simply gaze at some future contentment over the abyss of the actual, which is usually the way with desire, but has a foretaste of its fulfilment, mixing a certain euphoria with its sense of incompletion by discerning signs and pledges of the future within the present. Indeed, Christianity associates the condition with joyful anticipation. As Ernst Bloch puts it, 'The happy present is simultaneously grasped as pledge for the future.'[29] Desire, by contrast, is not for the most part agreeable. Those who desire do not smile and turn somersaults, as those who hope may do. This is because they are frustrated, as those who hope are not. Only if their hopes fail will they become so.

In Ludwig Wittgenstein's view, the temporal structure of hope involves language. 'One can imagine an animal angry, frightened, unhappy, happy, startled', he writes. 'But hopeful? And why not?'[30] It would be enough to point out, he argues, that it does not possess language. A dog, he remarks, may be vaguely expecting his master to return, but he cannot be expecting him to return at a precise time on a particular day, since as a nonlinguistic creature he lacks the concept of, say, Wednesday or three o'clock. On this view, only those who have acquired a language can be said to hope. It is language that opens up large future possibilities. Philo writes that hope is one of the most vital distinguishing features between humans and the other animals, but the case depends on the size of the aspirations in question. It is true that one cannot speak of a dog's secret ambition to resolve the Israeli-Palestinian conflict or enjoy a quiet candlelit dinner with Scarlett Johansson, but one can surely speak of its hope to be thrown a bone. Though it cannot expect its master to return at three o'clock, it can presumably feel a certain eager anticipation of nuzzling his face once again. Wittgenstein didn't like dogs, and was perhaps inclined to underestimate their capabilities.[31] Aquinas, who may have been fonder of dogs than Wittgenstein was, believed that like other animals they were capable of hope.[32]

A widespread preoccupation with hope is bound up with the historicism of the modern epoch. It is a key signifier in the transition from the tradition-bound to the future-oriented, from timeless metaphysical truths to the historically open-ended. This, at least, was how Martin Luther saw the matter. In his view, 'The philosophers fix their eyes on the presence of things, and reflect only on their qualities and quiddities. But the apostle [Paul] drags our gaze away from contemplating the present state of things, and directs it towards their future. He does not speak of the essence or the workings of the creature . . . but employs a new, strange, theological term and speaks of the expectation of the creature.'[33] Modernity is a question of viewing the present in the light of its future, and thus in the light of its potential negation. Essence is now expectation. What defines a phenomenon, in a reversal of linear evolution, is the inner form that inflects it toward the as yet unrealised. In a Benjaminesque inversion, it is its future that determines its present. And since it is the apostle Paul who proclaims this momentous truth, modernity might be thought to stretch back a surprisingly long way.

In the wake of Luther, Jürgen Moltmann observes that for the ancient Greeks truth is assured and eternal, whereas for the ancient Hebrews it resides in the tension between a divine promise and the historical redemption of it.[34] 'From first to last', he writes, 'Christianity is eschatology, is hope, forward-looking and forward-moving, and therefore also revolutionary and transforming the present.'[35] For the Jewish scriptures, claims Wolfhart

Pannenberg, all being has to be grasped as oriented toward the future. Eschatology, which involves 'the ontological primacy of the future in relation to the present', is in his view nothing less than the central category of Judeo-Christianity. 'God is not yet', he writes, 'but is yet to be.'[36] This predilection for the future is not, to be sure, an invariable feature of modern thought. Paul Ricoeur regards Hegel's writings as 'a philosophy of reminiscence' averse to the idea of hope, in contrast to Kant's vision of history.[37] Nicholas Boyle argues in similar vein that Hegel has no real philosophical concern with the future.[38]

It is tempting to see hope as an emotion or experience. Aristotle writes in his *Rhetoric* of it involving a pleasant sensation of its future object, rather as memory may do of some past event.[39] John Locke regards hope as the 'pleasure in the mind' we feel when anticipating some future source of enjoyment.[40] Ernst Bloch sometimes seems to regard it as an affect or emotion, as did René Descartes and David Hume. It ranks for Hume among the great central passions of fear, grief, joy, aversion and the like, and wells up when one contemplates a prospectively pleasurable event which is uncertain but not impossible.[41] Yet there is in fact no characteristic feeling, symptom, sensation or behaviour pattern associated with hope, as there is with rage or horror. This is partly because it is a species of desire; and though desire is an experience, it is associated with no definitive sensation or affect.[42] One can hope without feeling anything in particular. The same is true of expecting. A woman who is said to be 'expecting' does not spend every moment of the day eagerly anticipating the birth of her child. Wittgenstein points out that promising and intending are not experiences either. Nor, one might add, is belief, which like hope is a disposition rather than a sensation. As Wittgenstein seeks to demonstrate, we continually mistake dispositions or social practices for states of feeling. To make a promise while secretly resolving to break it, for example, is still to have promised, since promising is a social institution, not a mental act. To marry while privately dissociating oneself from the ceremony is still to have acquired a spouse. To say that one is intending to meet the

Prince of Wales next week is not to report on a state of mind but to describe a situation. Such an intention may well involve feelings (dread, panic, revulsion and the like), but it may not. Even if it does, it is not defined by them.

The same is true of hope, even though it can come wrapped in such emotional states as eagerness, excitement, anticipation and so on. Stan van Hooft points out that it makes perfect sense to say 'He has no hope of succeeding' even when the agent himself believes that he has. We are speaking here of a situation rather than an inward conviction.[43] To speak hopefully is to use words in a certain way, not to invest them with a particular affect. Even if one privately feels nothing but a spasm of savage nihilism in the act of consoling someone else, hopeful words remain hopeful words. To declare that one hopes to see a friend next week is not generally to claim that one is the subject of certain sensations. To announce one's hope for an end to child labour is more likely to be a political statement than a psychological one. As Jayne Waterworth wryly puts it, 'A woman's hoping for her husband's or son's return is not in some prolonged affective state for two weeks, months or years.'[44] Does her hoping cease the moment she claps eyes on her husband, like a suddenly assuaged stab of pain, or does it linger for a while before fading away? Is it still present when she is asleep, as an ache in the guts can be? If hope is a disposition rather than an emotion, one may indeed speak of someone as hopeful while they are asleep.[45] If you were callous enough to prod him in the chest and ask him whether he had hopes for world peace, and he grunted 'yes' in response, this could be said to settle the matter. One may recognise that a hope is real without having the least sensation of it. In fact, you may acknowledge that there are rational grounds for hope while feeling thoroughly suicidal, rather as the temperamentally cheerful can sometimes be brought to concede that a situation is irreparable.

The Oxford philosopher Gilbert Ryle, when asked by a colleague when he might hope to see his next book, is said to have replied, 'You may hope whenever you like.' It is a classic High

Table remark. No doubt Ryle, in suavely malicious style, was drawing attention to a grammatical ambiguity, and thus implicitly upbraiding his colleague for a kind of solecism. 'When may we hope to see your new book?' means of course 'When may we have the pleasure of seeing it?', not 'At what moment in time may we begin hoping that it will appear?' But Ryle might also have been doing some off-the-cuff philosophy. Perhaps he was making a point about the nature of hope by mischievously misinterpreting it as a voluntary affair (we cannot in fact simply hope whenever we like), or as a sensation whose onset we can gauge with some precision. To ask 'What do you hope to achieve?' is to request an account of a project, not a report on a subjective condition. It is the structure of intentionality inscribed in a situation, not an experience, which is at stake here. One can be mistaken about harbouring genuine hopes, as one cannot be mistaken about being in acute distress. One might discover, for example, that one is not in the least dejected by the dramatic implosion of one's expectations, since one had been unconsciously aware all along that the object of them was trivial or beyond reach. Or perhaps you were hoping because you imagined that it was expected of you to do so.

To call hope a virtue is to claim that it is a disposition rather than an experience. Aquinas describes the theological version of it as 'a disposition of spirit', though he contrasts this with common-or-garden hope, which he ranks along with fear, grief and joy among the principal emotions.[46] John Stuart Mill speaks of the virtue in Boy Scoutish fashion as a disposition that 'gives a spur to the faculties and keeps all the active energies in good working order'.[47] Descartes views hope as a disposition of the soul to be convinced that what one desires will come about. Like any virtue, it is an acquired habit of thinking, feeling and acting in a specific way. It must belong to a form of life rather than being simply a one-off event. There is a difference between being patient and possessing the virtue of patience. Someone who is sober only once in his life cannot lay claim to the virtue of temperance. Moreover, habits and capabilities are not experiences.

A habitually hopeful individual is not in the first place one who enjoys certain sensations, but one who is predisposed to act and respond affirmatively with regard to the future. To this extent, he or she resembles the optimist; but to practise the virtue of hope is not necessarily to assume with the optimist that things will work out well. Indeed, there is more merit to be accrued in maintaining one's hope when the outlook is dismal. Besides, the hopeful must be able to peer into the abyss of potential disaster, which the optimist is generally reluctant to do. They must also be able to give reasons for their hopefulness (a general faith in humanity, for example), whereas the temperamental optimist feels no need to justify his upbeat nature, and indeed is incapable of doing so rationally.

If hope were simply a feeling, it would not count as a virtue, as it does for both Augustine and Aquinas. You can be commended for having a virtue, but not on having a feeling, at least of a spontaneous kind. People who sweat blood to feel forgiveness can be congratulated on their efforts, but to be instinctively compassionate, however much it may issue in moral good, is not itself a moral achievement because it is not an achievement at all. It is because hope can be cultivated by practice and self-discipline that it is a question of merit. Ernst Bloch is right to maintain that hope must be learned. To call it a virtue is to claim among other things that it is conducive to human happiness. On this theory, we should be hopeful because it belongs to our self-fulfilment to be so. We ought to hope, at least when it is reasonable to do so, rather as we ought not to hack at our limbs with butcher's knives or fester with envy at the accomplishments of others. It is not an option or a subjective whim. Some commentators reject this claim on the grounds that hope is a mode of desire, and desire is not generally within our control. We do not usually choose what we want. Indeed, none of the three theological versions is primarily a matter of the will. Perhaps those who object to the idea that we ought to hope underestimate the extent to which it can be actively cultivated. Even if hope is an obligation, however, this does not mean that we have a duty to be perpetually cheerful, or to hope when it is plainly pointless to do so. It is true that there is a sense in which Christians are habitually hopeful, however desolate the situation may appear, but this is because they think it reasonable to be so because of the promise of the resurrection.

It is worth noting that hope is the kind of virtue that involves a cluster of equally creditable qualities: patience, trust, courage, tenacity, resilience, forbearance, perseverance, long-sufferance and the like. Luther defines it as 'spiritual courage'.[48] The philosopher Alain Badiou sees hope primarily in terms of patience and persistence, as 'a principle of tenacity, of obstinacy'.[49] It is a form of 'fidelity to fidelity', the way in which one sticks fast to one's faith through the most testing and turbulent of events. Temperamental optimism, by contrast, has no use for most of the virtues characteristically associated with hope. As a spontaneous affair, it sees no need to nurture such moral habits.

It is possible to distinguish hope and desire in general, as we have been doing, while acknowledging that the former in a broad sense is a mode of the latter. Roughly speaking, hope consists of desire plus expectancy. One can expect without desiring, but one cannot hope without desiring. You can hope for something which is at once praiseworthy and disagreeable (that the best player will win, for example, when it palpably isn't you), or both gratifying and unpleasant (being punished for one's crimes, for example), but there is no hoping without wanting. Despair negates hope but not desire: someone in despair can yearn to abandon this life in order to be reunited with a dead companion, as Jayne Waterworth points out. Though hope, as we have seen already, belongs to the class of desires we label rational, this is not to say that it is always benign or legitimate. It is a species of morally refined desire, as opposed to a simple appetite, but this does not mean that it need be moral in a positive sense of the term. You can hope for the extermination of everyone under the age of seven, or that reviewers who hatchet your books will rot in hell. The fact that we hope for what strikes us as desirable does not necessarily mean that it is, or even that we ourselves believe it to be worth having. We may recognise that what we hope for is worthless or pernicious while continuing to hope for it.

The latter point is worth underlining, since there is a widespread illusion that hope is somehow precious in itself. It is a deceptively affirmative term, like 'family', 'imagination' or 'future'. Aquinas, however, reminds us that there are false or malicious aspirations, a point that Ernst Bloch might profitably have kept in mind rather more than he does. Who is to say that the arrival of Godot may not prove catastrophic? The British national anthem records its hope that the monarch's enemies will be confounded, a curious sentiment for a supposedly Christian nation. Perhaps one reason we instinctively think of hope as positive is because it involves the imagination, a faculty that is viewed in a venerable Romantic tradition as an unequivocal good. But there are toxic uses of the imagination as well as wholesome ones. Genocide requires a skilful enough application of it.

Both hope and desire can be groomed and nourished, learning to take as their end what is objectively good; and in both cases this requires the intervention of reason. Reason does not enter the picture simply when it comes to the question of how to realise one's hopes or desires, as both Hobbes and Hume imagine; it must be present, however dimly, from the outset. Thucydides contrasts hope and reason, but too sharp an opposition between them is surely a mistake.[50] 'Is there any hope?' means 'Is it reasonable to hope?' For the most part, states of desire are cognitive in that they engage ideas. It is true that you can feel a nameless yearning, rather as you can feel afraid without any conception of what it is you fear; but you cannot feel a passionate longing for something of which you can give no account at all. This is not to deny that there are forms of desire with a low cognitive content (being seized by an urge to yawn, for example), and other modes of it (say, wanting to see a large number of bankers behind bars) of which this is far from true. Hope, similarly, may be purely banal, as when one hopes not to sneeze at the moment of one's death; or it can be a highly cognitive affair, involving knowledge, belief and understanding in the way that nausea or nameless irascibility do not.

It is this which Ernst Bloch calls *docta spes*. Hope of this kind is a moral orientation, not simply a wish or spontaneous impulse. Reason cannot blossom without hope, Bloch writes in *The Principle of Hope*, and hope cannot flourish without reason. Perhaps hope engages reason more deeply than some other modes of desire because, as we have seen, its end must be feasible, and such feasibility may call for fine judgment. We have also seen that hope involves a kind of plotting or projecting, in the sense of an imaginative articulation of present and future, and this, too, has its rational aspects. A baby may desire to be fed, but it cannot hope to be. Denys Turner writes of 'that power to thread a continuity of desire through often complex overlapping strands of rationally connected wants' which Aquinas calls *voluntas*, and which represents a richer conception of the will than the bloodless brand of voluntarism typical of modern times.[51] One might describe hope, too, in something like these terms.

If hope involves reason, what is one to make of Antonio Gramsci's celebrated political slogan 'Pessimism of the intellect, optimism of the will'? The maxim is a warning to the political left not to allow its clear-eyed estimate of the problems it confronts to sap its resolve. Yet is cognitive dissonance really the best policy? Are the two faculties quite so easily dissociable? They can, to be sure, be divorced to some degree. You might consider, for example, that things will turn out well but hope that they will not, which is more or less the opposite of what Gramsci recommends. In general, no doubt, Gramsci well understood that the will must be rationally informed if it is to issue in constructive action. Pressed too far, however, his battle cry is in danger of lapsing into voluntarism or even adventurism. It might also in the end prove strictly impossible. You can act positively even when you regard the situation as hopeless, but you cannot act hopefully if you regard it as hopeless.

Hope can be a high-minded, hand-on-heart term, but it can also be a more mundane, run-of-the-mill affair. 'In a general sense', Waterworth comments, 'hope is built into the very structure of agency.'[52] We can know that someone has hope not by investigating her inner life but by observing what she is doing. It is clear from the way she has just smashed the kitchen window that she is hoping to get into the house despite having mislaid her door key. A certain low-level, unreflective form of hope is rife throughout human existence, as is a certain unglamorous form of imagination. One would not raise the glass to one's lips unless one had a dim premonition, culled from previous experience, of the high probability of its arriving at its goal. It is in this sense that hope can be described as 'a fundamental existential structure of human existence'.[53]

For some commentators, however, there is a more absolute form of hope which keeps a lofty distance from such common-or-garden aspirations. In his *Homo Viator*, one of the most renowned of modern meditations on the virtue, the philosopher Gabriel Marcel, doyen of Christian existentialism, claims that hope 'tends inevitably to transcend the particular objects to which it at first seems to be attached',[54] which lends it an affinity to desire in the psychoanalytic sense. Desire, too, is a mode of transcendence, a secularised version of the absolute as radically homeless and otherworldly as the Almighty himself. For psychoanalytic theory, all particular wants are infiltrated by a fundamental longing that appears to be purely intransitive, and that can thus never be assuaged. For Christianity, this deep, unconditional craving represents the way human beings are oriented to their Creator and will find their fulfilment only when they come to rest in him. It is the trace of his presence in the structure of their being, the subtext of all specific cravings. 'All our natural hopes', writes the theologian Josef Pieper, 'tend toward fulfilments that are like vague mirrorings and foreshadowings of, like unconscious preparations for, eternal life.'[55] We shall see later that Ernst Bloch's philosophy represents a profane version of this Pauline vision. Bloch, writes one of his commentators, 'is the historian of the pre-appearance of absolute or total hope in particular hopes'.[56]

If the most trifling of hopes is secretly animated by a utopian impulse, so the most banal of desires might be said to secrete a certain sublimity at its heart. Psychoanalysis inherits from religious faith the concept of an unconditional desire but abolishes its transcendent object-source, thus converting the comedy of Christian faith into what can be seen as a tragic vision. It is now not God, but the unslakeable desire for him (in Lacanian terms, the desire of the Real), to which we pledge our fidelity, a desire that can be as absolute and implacable as any deity. In this sense, a yearning for God has assumed some of the qualities which are traditionally thought to characterise him. For Marcel, absolute hope is an infinite, unconditional capacity that exceeds all particular objects and can only be degraded by being subject to representation. 'Hope', Marcel writes, 'consists in asserting that there is at the heart of being, beyond all data, beyond all inventories and calculations, a mysterious principle which is in connivance with me.'[57] It is hard to see how this has a bearing on such workaday sentiments as hoping for good weather or a change in the interest rate.

What Marcel calls absolute hope is not based on experience, indeed takes no account of it, and rises from the ruins of all specific aspirations. It disdains all rational calculation, sets itself no limit or condition, preserves an unshakeable assurance, and is immune to disappointment, subsisting 'in a zone of utter metaphysical security' (48). As such, it represents a rebuff to history, not an audacious openness to it. Since it stands free of material conditions and can never be dashed, it is hard to see how it differs from pathological optimism. This brand of hope, with its triumphalist air, sounds rather too close for comfort to presumption.

It comes as no surprise, then, that *Homo Viator* was written by a patriotic French intellectual during the Nazi occupation of his country, at a time when the hope of the populace could easily decline into a vein of wishful thinking or dream of indomitability. It is impossible, Marcel declares, not to believe that France will one day be free, since despair would be disloyal. One must hope, he insists, 'in the teeth of will and knowledge' (67). This, then, is the equivalent in the realm of hope of fideism in the domain of faith. 'Hope and the calculating faculty of reason', Marcel insists, 'are essentially distinct' (65). Reason, being a question of instrumental rationality, can have no truck with so august a virtue. Because it is insulated from the empirical sphere, and thus incapable of being discouraged, absolute hope for Marcel signifies a kind of certitude. It represents not only a repudiation of history but a disavowal of tragedy. Rather than passing through tragic dissolution, it soars dispassionately above it. A mother who hopes that her son is alive when everyone else knows him to be dead, writes Marcel, has a hope 'beyond the reach of objective criticism' (66). To suggest that it would be kinder in the long run to tell the mother the truth would no doubt be in this view an ignoble capitulation to circumstance. What *Homo Viator* really promotes in such passages is hope as ideology. It is a quasi-religious way of cheering oneself up, grandly impervious to all counterargument. Rather as there is no authentic faith that is not open to doubt, so a hope that cannot falter would seem too much like definitive knowledge to figure as hope at all. This is not a faith or hope held in fear and trembling. It is not one that can take with full seriousness Jesus's lament to his Father on the cross.

Marcel is wary of the idea of specific or definitive hope because it is too drably empirical, rather as the messianism of the later Derrida would be confounded were the Messiah to do anything as drearily determinate as to arrive. It is the privileged view of those who have no need of any very palpable form of redemption, and for whom the idea of hope as a perpetual, open-ended anticipation of nothing in particular is therefore likely to exert some appeal. Hope must remain contentless if it is not to be blighted. The only Messiah who is likely not to let us down is the one who never shows up.

To sustain his trust that the Nazis will one day be routed,

Marcel needs to nourish a hope so unswerving and implacable that it can survive all confounding because it is nothing in particular. The only viable form of hope in such cheerless times must be one without a name. 'Hope's time', writes Andrew Benjamin in similar vein, 'will become the opening—an intense present—holding the present as always opening, as always being the irreconcilable.'[58] The awkwardness of the grammar reflects the smokiness of the thought. Are openness and irreconcilability unqualified goods? Are they being proposed as absolute values? Openness to a future of slavery, or irreconcilability to nonracism? The original Jewish promise is not of this nebulous kind. It is a promise of justice to the poor and freedom to the oppressed, a vision which poststructuralist thinkers like Benjamin are likely to find distastefully determinate. He is wary of what he calls a 'policy and practice of accomplishments',[59] though those in need of a few tangible proposals to improve their condition might take a different view.

Even so, there is a kind of indeterminate hope that is not so vague as to be vacuous. It is this which Marcel calls fundamental rather than absolute hope. Such hope acknowledges the realities of failure and defeat, but refuses to capitulate in the face of them and preserves an unspecified, nonpurposive openness to the future.[60] St Paul speaks of hope as reaching 'even beyond the veil', meaning that what we reach out to is concealed from us. It is not a question à la Derrida of openness for its own sake, since one is able to spell out something of its contents. The object of Paul's hope may be elusive, but at least he can give it the name of God. Even so, it follows from his words that Christians can never define exactly what it is they are hoping for. Strangely enough, the hope itself is certain, as we shall see in a moment, but its object is obscure. Ernst Bloch holds likewise that what we hope for is ultimately unknown to us. The Epistle to the Hebrews speaks of Abraham being called forth in faith 'not knowing where he is going', which combines the determinate with the indistinct in the manner of St Paul. In similar vein, Kant writes in *Religion Within the Limits of Reason Alone* of one 'who trusts without knowing how that which he hopes for will come to pass'.[61] The trust is unshakeable but the mode of attainment is not. There is a difference between doubting whether one's hope will be fulfilled, as in the phrase 'I hope so' (with the tacit rider 'but I'm not sure'), and a confident commitment to a future that outstrips one's comprehension. Leibniz speaks of a form of inarticulate knowledge in which we know and don't know something simultaneously, or know it potentially rather than actually. One is gratified to note that the former US Defense Secretary Donald Rumsfeld, with his celebrated talk of 'known unknowns', was in this sense a devoted Leibnizian, though the fact was almost certainly unknown to him.[62] It is a condition close to Paul's conception of faith and hope. If we knew exactly what we were hoping for when we speak of a different future, it would not be sufficiently remote from what we see around us, and thus not different enough. Perhaps we will only know what to hope for when the object of our hope is finally unveiled, as there is a sense for psychoanalysis in which we are instructed in what to desire.[63]

T. S. Eliot writes in *Four Quartets* of waiting without hope for fear that hope would be hope for the wrong thing. It is an idea close to the Heideggerian concept of *Gelassenheit*, or Marcel's notion of 'active waiting', whereby one casts aside any strenuous project or definitive object for a vulnerable openness to what the world may come up with. Indeterminacy of this sort is bound up with a precious kind of passivity. Eliot's lines may spurn hope, but they remain committed all the same to a somewhat featureless state of waiting. Reality is dimmed down so that possibility may be lit up, as in these delectable lines from John Keats's 'Ode to a Nightingale':

> I cannot see what flowers are at my feet,
> Nor what soft incense hangs upon the boughs,
> But, in embalmed darkness, guess each sweet
> Wherewith the seasonable month endows
> The grass, the thicket, and the fruit-tree wild,

White hawthorn, and the pastoral eglantine;
Fast-fading violets cover'd up in leaves;
And mid-May's eldest child,
The coming must rose, full of dewy wine,
The murmurous haunt of flies on summer eves.

D. H. Lawrence ('one of the penis pets', as Bloch priggishly calls him) is also much taken with this stance of reverent receptivity, one that refuses to foist its own ends and interests on the world but is prepared, as in the Keatsian doctrine of negative capability, to wait humbly in darkness and ambiguity for some unchartable new current of life to stir, without any anxious reaching out for ontological security. For Lawrence, the self is not something we can possess, but a process that manifests its own strange logic and evolves in its own sweet way. If courage is an active virtue, then having the audacity to let oneself go is to live in a curiously oxymoronic state. Rupert Birkin in *Women in Love* is prepared to let everything pass away, in the faith that some new, magnificent dispensation of being will emerge from its ruins. Ursula Brangwen finds herself in this fertile, disconsolate condition at the end of *The Rainbow*. Eric Fromm writes that 'to hope means to be ready at every moment for that which is not yet born, and yet not become desperate if there is no birth in our lifetime'.[64]

In *The Principle of Hope*, Ernst Bloch, who believes likewise that the self is not a possession, sees the present moment as elusive and unreadable, a surplus that eludes the concept, and in this sense as a dim prefiguring of the future. We have a foretaste of the future in our very inability to seize the impenetrable present or unpack the enigma of the self. If we were indeed able to 'bite the day to the core', in Edward Thomas's pregnant phrase, we would doubtless find ourselves in the presence not of the future but of eternity. Perhaps leisure, which bucks the tyranny of time, is one of our closest approximations to it. In Bloch's view, the 'now' can be lived but not grasped, and it is in this felt opacity – this gap between the experiential and the conceptual – that the shadowy profile of the future can be discerned. Fredric Jameson detects a similar hiatus in Proust, for whom the raw material of the present must be recollected in tranquility, mediated by art and language, if *Erlebnis* is to be converted into *Erfahrung* and experience lived through for real as though for the first time.[65]

Perhaps the Lawrentian dark night of the soul, strictly speaking, is more a matter of faith than hope. Yet hope is for the most part the future tense of faith, 'faith in relation to the future' as Feuerbach puts it;[66] and if one can be vigilant in this way to what may spring unpredictably into being, which is a question of faith, it is because of a trust that there will indeed be such fresh stirrings of life, which is a matter of hope. The two virtues are closely intertwined, and both have their foundation in charity. It is the assurance of being loved that enables one to take the risk of faith, a faith that in turning its face to the future melts into hope.[67]

The theologian Karl Rahner sees hope as a radical abandonment of the self, a commitment to what one acknowledges to be beyond one's control and calculation. In this sense, too, hope resembles faith, and like faith poses a challenge to the ethic of self-possession. It allows one to enter upon the incalculable, as the familiar yields to the unknown. It is a version of what Lawrence calls the 'endless venture into consciousness'. As Raymond Williams observes in *Culture and Society, 1780–1950*, 'We have to plan what can be planned, according to our common decision. But the emphasis of the idea of culture is right when it reminds us that a culture, essentially, is unplannable. We have to ensure the means of life, and the means of community. But what will then, by these means, be lived, we cannot know or say.'[68] The past can be grasped as an achieved reality, but the future can be known only *ambulando*, in the process of constructing it. Like the theologians, incidentally, Williams takes it for granted that hope is in the first place not hope for oneself but hope for us.

In Rahner's view, there is a politics implicit in the self-abandonment which hope involves. By fostering trust, hope allows us 'constantly to undertake an exodus out of the present into the future'.[69] 'To subject the structures of the world to constant reappraisal and criticism', he writes, 'is one of the concrete forms of Christian hope which, as the courage of self-commitment to the incalculable and uncontrollable, must never hold fast to anything in the worldly life in a way that it is thought without it man would be cast headlong into an absolute void.'[70] Hope divests all times to come of their false appearance as absolute futures. For Rahner, there is indeed an absolute future (the kingdom of God), but its role is to defetishise whatever else we might look expectantly to, along with what has been accomplished already. Hope is thus a species of permanent revolution, whose enemy is as much political complacency as metaphysical despair. Because there is in principle no end to it, it refuses to make an idol out of any specific setup, which is not to say that it refuses to judge among them. As Jürgen Moltmann comments, hope keeps us radically unreconciled to the present, thus figuring as a constant source of historical disruption.[71] The more conservative theologian John Macquarrie, by contrast, is wary of the future-oriented bias of hope precisely on the grounds that it might encourage 'unrealistic and utopian hopes'.[72] Too much loose talk of the future gives comfort to the political left, even if a scepticism of utopian hope comes oddly from one who presumably believes in the general resurrection.

If there is a passive aspect to hope, its opposite in this respect is not so much despair as pure self-determination. What need is there for hope when one can be author of oneself? The ancient Stoics, who sought to exercise complete mastery over themselves, saw hope as involving both dependency and incompleteness, and so viewed it with suspicion. *King Lear* is all about ripeness, patience and endurance, whereas dedicated self-fashioners like Macbeth and Coriolanus, who seek to be sole agents of their own destiny, reject all dependency as ignoble. Shakespeare's villains are typically impervious to being acted on. Hope, by contrast, recalls us to what rebuffs our dominion. To say 'I hope to do so' is to concede that there are limits to one's power. Hope and humility are in this sense bedfellows. 'We must remember', writes Epicurus, 'that the future is neither wholly ours nor wholly not ours, so that neither must we count upon it as quite certain to come nor despair of it as quite certain not to come.'[73] Those guilty of the sin of presumption seek to possess the future, while those in despair abandon all effort to bring it to birth. If hope marks a limit to human powers, it is partly because it is not finally a question of the will. Just as we do not choose to desire, so, by and large, we do not choose to hope. It is true that we can sometimes persuade ourselves into feeling positive on a particular issue, rather as one can suppress one's hopes because they are unrealistic or morally unacceptable, or because achieving them might involve too much sweated labour. One might decide that it would be imprudent to hope, or simply not worth it. In this sense, you can decide to hope rather as you can decide to sulk, or as you can try to stop yourself falling in love. Immanuel Kant's question 'What may I hope for?' can be taken to imply that hope lies within one's control. There is, however, a limit to this capacity. Hope is not a state of affairs we can easily turn on and off, any more than envy or disgust.

Marcel's absolute hope may be a form of ideology, but there is a more suggestive sense in which hope may be unconditional. This is the view that though this or that aspiration might come to nothing, it is reasonable to retain an underlying confidence in humanity as such. Since the future is unpredictable, it is rash to dismiss the possibility that some unfathomable good may emerge in the fullness of time, or even in the next twenty-four hours. Think, for example, of the extraordinary opening decade of the twenty-first century. There were plenty of commentators around the turn of the century, in the triumphalist climate of the West's victory in the Cold War and its still relatively robust economy, who were to be found arguing that history was over, epochal events exhausted, large-scale alternatives to the status quo discredited, and grand narratives washed up. The future would be simply a reprise of the present. Precisely at that point, the World Trade Center collapsed, a so-called war on terror was launched, a financial crisis of spectacular proportions rocked the capitalist world, a number of autocrats were dethroned, and a range of populations rose en masse against their rulers. It is not that these events are bound to issue in some signal improvement. It is rather that they demonstrate the folly of trusting to what Martin Luther would see as certain timeless imperatives rather than to the gamble of history. If timeless imperatives were metaphysical for Martin Luther, they were ideological for the end-of-history merchants. For Bertolt Brecht, by contrast, the mere fact of change, even change for the worse, is a prophylactic against despair, since if history can decline it can also advance.

Fundamental hope is what one is thrown back on when all specific hopes have failed, rather as desire for psychoanalytic theory is what remains once one has subtracted from it all specific demands. It is thus not always easy to distinguish from despair. Absolute despair, however, is a question of shedding not this or that hope, but hope as such. Indeed, Kierkegaard holds that all despair is in some sense absolute, and that not to acknowledge this fact is a form of false consciousness. 'He thinks he is in despair over something earthly', he remarks, 'and yet his despair is of the eternal.'[74] Yet just as there is a metaphysical vein of despair, so there is an unconditional form of hope. As José Saramago writes in *The Year of the Death of Ricardo Reis*: 'To hope, hope in what, Hope, just hope, one reaches a point where there is nothing but hope, and that is where we discover that hope is everything.' There is, the novel implies in Marcelian style, a kind of pure, intransitive hope, a fundamental bias or built-in inclination of one's being, which comes fully to light only when all actual aspirations have been stripped away.

This, one might claim, is a tragic view, which is not necessarily to say a pessimistic one. Tragedy is concerned with what, if anything, survives when humanity has been hacked down to almost nothing. Whatever residue then remains, whatever still refuses to give way, is what can assuredly be built upon. It is thus that nothing veers on its axis to become something. As Ross puts it in *Macbeth*, 'Things at the worst will cease, or else climb up / To what they were before' (act 4, scene 1). In *Hope and History*, Josef Pieper argues rather similarly that there is a fundamental form of hope that comes into focus only with the possibility of absolute despair, in the sense of a rejection of human existence as such. Only then, beyond all specific hopes and in full awareness of their fragility, can this pure essence of hope manifest itself. 'Hope', writes Gabriel Marcel, '. . . can only take root where perdition is a possibility.'[75] This is one of the several ways in which it differs from optimism, for which perdition is simply inconceivable. The Abraham who takes a knife to his son's throat has hope, but one would hesitate to describe him as an optimist.

The kind of despair which Christianity ranks as sinful is a matter of rejecting the long-term possibility of redemption, not of concluding that this or that particular effort is clearly doomed. One reason why despair of this longer-term kind is considered a moral defect is that it can be seen as betraying the efforts of others. It may suggest that their apparent victories are bogus and their failures foredoomed, thus belittling their courage and resilience. One may abandon a specific situation as lost, then, while retaining an unspecific trust in the future, which is what Marcel means by fundamental hope. Such hope has no particular objective, but is rather a question of a general openness of spirit – what one commentator calls 'a tone or disposition with which one faces the future . . . a simple steadfastness or an objectless expectancy'.[76] It differs from optimism partly because it is not merely a question of temperament, and partly because it is ready to confront the possibility of its own ruin. Perhaps this fundamental species of hope is what persuades us that even in the midst of calamity, life is still worth living. It may be no more than a question of wishing to persist – not for the sake of anything in particular, but because such persistence is the precondition of coming to want or achieve something particular. Life is a necessary if not sufficient condition of hope. Fundamental or unconditional hope is thus a kind of meta-hope, the transcendental possibility of all our more palpable aspirations.

When asked by his friend Max Brod whether there was any hope beyond the world with which we are familiar, Franz Kafka is said to have replied that there was an abundance, even an infinity of it – 'but not for us'. Perhaps he meant that the universe as we know it is a bad mood of God's, created on an off day, and that had his temper at the time been less dyspeptic, things on earth might have been considerably less dire. Or perhaps he meant that there are other worlds in which things are considerably less dire at this very moment. Humanity might have missed the possibility of redemption by a minuscule misalignment of the cosmic forces. One is reminded of the mystical Jewish belief that when the Messiah arrives, he will transform everything by making a few minor adjustments. In one sense, Kafka's claim renders our situation more poignant, since there might indeed have been grounds for hope; in another sense, it tempers that pathos by implying that there might be hope in plenty elsewhere. 'Plenty of hope, but not for us' might well be the motto of some of Chekhov's characters, who look to a future felicity from which they know they will be excluded.

Those who take their own life are often said to be in despair. Yet this needs to be more finely nuanced. Someone who commits suicide need not be convinced that there is no value to existence as such. On the contrary, she may believe that there is every reason to hope, but that such expectations are not for her. Or she may see that there is reason for her to hope, but not feel that there is. She might consider that her problems could vanish, but find herself unable to wait that long. The pain is too unbearable for her to attend on some more benign turn of events. Gabriel Marcel speaks of despair as a form of impatience, but that someone is unable to wait any longer may be plain realism. The act of suicide, then, need not imply some absolute despair, either for oneself or for humanity in general, which is not to deny that there are circumstances in which absolute despair, in the sense of an unqualified rejection of hope, may be entirely rational. To succumb to such a state is often regarded as a moral weakness, but there are occasions when it is surely the last word in clear-sightedness. A doctor may reasonably despair of curing a terminally ill patient.

Suicide is a matter of hope. You kill yourself in the expectation of ceasing to suffer. One can even hope for the destruction of the entire human race, in the manner of the political philosopher John Gray. '*Homo sapiens*', he writes, 'is only one of very many species, and not obviously worth preserving. Later or sooner, it will become extinct. When it is gone the Earth will recover. Long after the traces of the human animal have disappeared, many of the species it is bent on destroying will be still around, along with others that have yet to spring up. The Earth will forget mankind. The play of life will go on.'[77] For Christianity, hope finally stretches beyond the human, though not beyond the human species itself, which it does for Gray. Anticipating one's own nonexistence may bring with it a strange kind of peace, as it does with Schopenhauer. It involves a dispassionate abnegation of the self which is close to the aesthetic. On this view, the most precious form of hope is one for a situation in which all hope has become impossible, since there is no one left to be the subject of it. This need not be a counsel of despair. On the contrary, when humanity has withered away, life can come into its own, freed of this passing impediment to its flourishing. D. H. Lawrence took a similar view.

Fundamental hope clings to a nameless conviction that life is ultimately worth living. Yet it is not certain that this is so. As Schopenhauer is brazen enough to point out, there are a great many men and women who would probably have been better off dead than alive. There might well be circumstances (a nuclear wasteland and an irredeemably poisoned planet, for example) in which when it comes to carrying on as a species, the kicks would clearly outweigh the ha'pence. Life is not precious in itself, in the sense that it is not self-evidently preferable to be alive rather than dead. Someone in chronic, atrocious pain is unlikely to believe so. It is not true that where there's life there's hope, though the opposite is surely the case. A humanity condemned to a future of torment and destitution, with no plausible hope of an alternative, might well think it better to blow the whistle on the whole ill-starred enterprise. To this extent, the idea of fundamental hope may turn out to be unfounded, at least outside a religious context; though the fact that we cannot know this for sure, since we cannot foresee the future, may help to sustain it. We shall see later, however, that it is possible to be hopeless yet not to despair.

༄༅

What it is to despair, however, is as vexed an issue as what it is to hope. It is not the same as feeling desperate, since as J. P. Day points out, despair tends to take the form of fatalistic inertia, and desperation of frantic activity. To despair is to do nothing about your situation, whereas to be desperate is to be prepared to do almost anything.[78] In his great phenomenology of despair, *The Sickness Unto Death*, Søren Kierkegaard portrays the condition in terms that anticipate the culture of postmodernism. As one who accomplishes the improbable task of raising Protestantism to the dignity of a philosophy, Kierkegaard sees individuals as summoned by God to the arduous project of becoming them-selves, a project that involves grounding themselves, each in his or her inimitable way, in his own unfathomable Being. It is hard to capture the full force of his wonder at the very idea of the indi-vidual self, which figures for him both as triumph and as terror. It is constituted by the absolute claim that God makes on each of us from all eternity—by the mind-shaking fact that his Son suffered and died for *me*, that my selfhood is as irreducible and *sui generis* as the universe itself, that I stagger under the appalling, exhila-rating burden of being responsible for this utterly unique entity known as myself, which will ever only occur once in the whole measureless stretch of cosmic time and which I, and I alone, am charged with bringing to either paradise or perdition.

Laden with this crippling obligation, it is not surprising that men and women should flee from it to some less sublimely in-timidating form of identity, refusing to become the self to which they have been eternally summoned and turning instead to some more gratifying, ready-to-hand mode of existence. Self-fashion-ing subjects of this kind despair of appropriating the selfhood that is truly theirs – one that is, so to speak, laid up in heaven for them – and opt instead for various fantastical, hypothetical, off-the-peg forms of identity, conjuring themselves arbitrarily

75

into existence in what Kierkegaard calls a 'fictional' mode, then whimsically dissolving themselves to nothing. Like the post-modern subject, they are clay in their own hands, intoxicated with pure possibility. Such men and women yearn to be sovereign over themselves; but since the self has been volatilised away, they find themselves in the unenviable position of absolute monarchs without a country. And this is to live in a kind of despair. In Kierkegaard's eyes, the contradiction these men and women cannot stomach is that genuine human autonomy is founded on a dependence on God – a dependence which like any other form of givenness or constraint, determinacy or necessity, these arrogantly libertarian spirits can regard only as an intolerable impediment. They cannot accept the fact that we do not belong to ourselves, and that only on this foundation can any authentic identity flourish. It is, incidentally, a belief enough in itself to refute any view of Kierkegaard as an 'existentialist'.

Yet individuals plunged into this plight are unable to elude their true or eternal selves entirely, a fact which for Kierkegaard then breeds a different form of despair. Because they want to be what they are not, they end up not wanting to be at all. What they yearn for is death; but death in Kierkegaard's view is out of the question, since the core of the self is eternal. Death is hope for the believer but hell for those in despair. 'The hopelessness [of despair]', Kierkegaard writes, 'is that even the last hope, death, is gone.'[79] Pressed to an extreme, this urge to be shot of life takes a demonic form. It is the condition of those who rage against the sheer fact of existence, disgusted by the scandal that there is anything at all, and as such in revolt against what Thomas Aquinas would see as the inherent goodness of Being.[80] These demoniacs are cynics and nihilists for whom the very notion of meaning is an outrage, the very idea of value bankrupt and fraudulent. Seized by a sullen fury against the world, they behave like spiteful infants bitterly disenchanted with their bungling parents. If they long for annihilation, however, they are also intent on staying alive in order to spit in God's eye and rub his nose in the farcical futility of his Creation, of which they themselves are among the most eye-catching examples.

This perverse form of despair, Kierkegaard comments,

does not even want to sever itself defiantly from the power that established it [i.e., God]; it wants in sheer spite to press itself on that power, importune it, hang on to it out of malice . . . Rebelling against all existence, it thinks it has acquired evidence against existence, against its goodness. One in despair thinks that he himself is that evidence, and it is this that he wants to be: this is the reason he wants to be himself, to be himself in his agony, so as to protest with this agony against all existence.[81]

Comfort, in a word, would be the undoing of the damned. It is their obscenely gratifying vindictiveness that keeps them in existence. The doomed cling to their torment like a child to its blanket, exulting in their agony, despising all offers of salvation as an affront to their spiritual dignity, and preferring a life of anguish to the horror of nonbeing. It is as though their inability to die is the nothingness at the core of the self which sustains it in ersatz existence. It is sickness and self-violence that keep them afloat.

If one kind of despair consists in drowning in possibility, another lies in spurning it altogether. In Kierkegaard's view, there is a void of the Real at the core of the self which is where God makes his presence felt, and to confront this fearful abyss is the only way through to hope. Those who greet this sublime vacancy with dread, however, can always find refuge from it in the false consciousness of the masses. 'There are very few people', he remarks, 'who live their lives to any degree at all in the category of spirit.'[82] Most men and women exist in a state of unreflective immediacy, whereas for the finely self-conscious few, the self is pitched into perpetual crisis. The masses turn their backs on the risks and gambles of selfhood, incapable of that perilous venture into consciousness which is faith, and take their cue instead from conventional social mores. In a commodifying of the spirit, each individual is 'ground as smooth as a pebble, as exchangeable as a coin of the realm'.[83] It is the domain of Heidegger's *das Man* or

Sartre's *mauvaise foi*, in which men and women are scarcely aware enough of themselves as unique subjects to experience despair at all. For Kierkegaard, however, despair can be an objective as well as a subjective condition. To live in immediacy and illusion is to be bereft of hope, and to be ignorant of the fact is a symptom of that sickness. Indeed, despair in this sense is in Kierkegaard's eyes a mass phenomenon, as familiar as rain or sunshine. There are many who think themselves content but who are actually in dire straits, rather as one can believe oneself to be in good health but in fact be terminally ill. In Kierkegaard's view, it is as though most people on the planet are afflicted by an invisible ailment of which they are entirely unaware, not least because it passes under the name of happiness.

There is a consensus among theorists that one cannot hope for what one is sure will happen.[84] Hope and knowledge would seem to be mutually exclusive, rather as faith and knowledge are for the fideist heresy. The phrase 'I hope so' generally implies uncertainty. It is weaker than 'I think so', which in turn of course is less emphatic than 'I know'. Hope for Spinoza is always mixed with fear precisely because its object is obscure. Thomas Hardy writes in *Far from the Madding Crowd* of 'faith sinking to hope', meaning, presumably, that faith is something less than knowledge and hope an even more fragile disposition than faith.

There is, to be sure, a problem with the phrase 'what one is sure will happen'. In a nondeterministic universe there is no such thing as what is going to happen, in the sense of what will inevitably come about whatever we choose to do. This is one reason why God, who is said to have knowledge of the future, cannot know what will take place in Dallas next Monday at 6.27 pm, in the sense of knowing what is bound to take place then. In an open-ended world, there is no such object of knowledge; and if God knows the world then he must know it as it is, in its freedom, autonomy and contingency. He cannot know what will inevitably occur in much the same sense that he cannot know what a puce-coloured concept or a right-wing bottle of Burgundy would look like. Being omniscient, he knows for sure what will contingently happen in Dallas next Monday, but that is a different matter. As we shall see in a moment, he also knows for sure that his kingdom will come, but that is not like knowing that there is a tornado brewing up or an economic crisis waiting in the wings.

Even in some less hard-nosed sense of the phrase 'what is going to happen', however, it is not clear that to be sure of what will happen means that one cannot hope for it as well. Take the brand of scientific socialism rife in the late nineteenth century, for which the arrival of a socialist future was assured by certain ironclad historical laws, and was therefore an object of cognitive certainty. This surely did not mean that one might not still hope for that future, in the sense of looking to it with eager expectancy, being restless for its arrival, and continuing to cling to this certitude in the midst of doubts. 'Even though things look bad, I retain my conviction that they will work out' blends hope with a degree of certainty. An Althusserian might claim that one might possess certain knowledge at the level of science or theory, but still feel hopeful from the standpoint of ideology. Perhaps one can hope for what one thinks is bound to happen rather as one can feel remorse for a past that one acknowledges to be unalterable.

Christians see the advent of the kingdom of God as a matter of certainty, but they still regard hoping for it as a virtue. Unlike the common-or-garden use of the phrase 'I hope so', they place their trust in something they are sure will come about. Hope for St Paul means waiting patiently, joyfully and confidently for the coming of the Messiah. Leibniz's hope is based on his cosmic optimism, and is thus unassailable. Since a merciful deity has ordered all things to a beneficent end, hope is a question of tranquil assurance. In more secular mode, Condorcet dreams of a future of peace, equality and human perfection, while regarding the advent of such a social order as virtually certain.[85] The everyday use of the phrase, by contrast, qualifies any such sure expectation, rather as the words 'no doubt' have come to modify their literal meaning ('No doubt he scrubbed the jacket several times, but the bloodstains were still clearly visible') and 'surely' has acquired an interrogative rather than authoritative ring ('Surely you're not claiming that he never scrubbed the jacket at all?'). The philosopher Alain Badiou speaks with impeccable theological orthodoxy of hope in terms of certainty, and faith in terms of conviction.[86] He grasps the point that theologically speaking, faith does not mean 'I believe so, but I'm not sure'. So does his Parisian colleague Jean-Luc Nancy, who writes that 'faith is not belief . . . Faith is trust, and trust in the strongest sense, which is to say, a trust that cannot ultimately be explained or justified. And yet all trust is somehow justified, because otherwise there would be no reason to trust one thing rather than another . . . Faith is holding to an assurance about which nothing is sure.'[87]

The *Oxford English Dictionary* defines hope as a feeling of expectation and desire, but says nothing of uncertainty. The sole reference to hope in the Nicene Creed – *expecto resurrectionem mortuorum et vitam venturi saeculi* – does not allow for the possibility that the resurrection of the dead and eternal life might not materialise. The verb *expecto*, meaning to look to or look out for, carries no undertone of doubt. To say 'I hope to see you tomorrow' generally means that you look forward to doing so, not that you have grave doubts as to whether you will.

If this view is unacceptable to a philosopher like Jacques Derrida, it is because he can see certainty only as a matter of scientific calculation, rather as postmodernism can view it only as dogmatism. If one could count on what is coming, Derrida argues in *Specters of Marx*, hope would be a calculative, programmatic affair. But there is no reason to pay the positivists the compliment of taking on board their reified version of rationality, if only to proceed to reject it. There are many forms of certainty beyond those promoted by the scientific rationalists: Bonaventure speaks of hope in terms of 'the security of a certain trustfulness' rather than of self-evident knowledge.[88] It is true, as Paul Ricoeur suggests, that 'between hope and absolute knowledge we have to choose',[89] but this does not mean that anything short of absolute knowledge must be surrendered to the sceptics. One can be certain that one is in love, or that Bach is a finer composer than Liam Gallagher, or that torturing babies is not the most morally resplendent of acts. Derrida is a full-blooded fideist who regards certitude as inimical to both faith and hope. But faith and certitude only need be at daggers drawn if one subscribes to a bugbearish version of the latter. Nicholas Lash points out that Karl Popper's *The Poverty of Historicism* falsely identifies certainty with scientific predictability, confining it to explanation rather than interpretation.[90] Christianity, by contrast, teaches that faith is something less than complete knowledge, but is nevertheless a form of certainty. It is true that one must make do with faith in God because one cannot yet encounter him face to face, but this is not the same as treating a proposition as hypothetical because it cannot yet be scientifically verified. Abraham's faith in God is not a matter of subscribing to the theory that there exists a Supreme Being despite the evidence for the claim being inconclusive. He would doubtless have found any such conception unintelligible. To have faith in the capacity of men and women to resist injustice is not a question of supposing that such a capacity exists. Indeed, one might accept that it exists while having not the slightest faith in its robustness.

We do not generally speak of having faith or hope in a set of scientific propositions. Knowledge of this kind would seem both faithless and hopeless. It has no obvious truck with trust, commitment, desire, or conviction. Nobody's identity is at stake in the claim that there are no married bachelors, or that the vulcanologists have once again successfully predicted the eruption of Mount Etna. These are not situations in which we put ourselves at risk. We may courageously place our lives in the hands of aeronautical engineers, but not in the hands of Assyriologists. It is then easy to imagine that if there is a distinction between faith or hope and scientific demonstrability, the former must be no more than tentative speculations. Nobody who believes in socialism or feminism could conceivably make this mistake, though a good many socialists and feminists make it about Christianity. In any case, the philosopher C. S. Peirce argues that the process of acquiring knowledge involves hope in the progress of intellectual activity itself, and that in this sense hope is one of the 'indispensable requirements of logic'.[91]

We tend to suppose that those in despair are gripped by a sense of certitude, however regrettable or ill-founded, but not those who hope. Yet the Anglican funeral service speaks of the 'sure and certain' hope of resurrection. Rudolf Bultmann and Karl Heinrich Rengsdorf write of 'confident waiting and trustful hope'.[92] The truth is that Christians have hope not because the future is obscure but because it is in some inscrutable sense well-founded. The source of their hope lies in the Yahweh who identifies himself in the future tense in the Hebrew scriptures ('I shall be what I shall be'), and who will not fail his people. Hope in this sense is not a question of wishful thinking but of joyful expectation, one which is all the more admirable in circumstances where it seems hard to sustain. It represents what Jane Austen in *Persuasion* calls 'a cheerful confidence in futurity'. The Psalms promise that hope shall not be confounded, while St Paul insists that it does not delude us. A commentator on Thomas Aquinas describes his view of hope as involving an 'unshakeable confidence [and] vibrant assurance' that is remote from facile optimism, 'a restless and impatient expectancy, marked with verve and steadfastness, with the certainty of victory'.[93] Lest that final phrase sound unpleasantly self-satisfied, one should recall that presumption for Christian faith is as much a sin as despair. It is the theological equivalent of pathological optimism. It is the faith that salvation is ultimately in God's hands, but that God's ways are mysterious ones, that allows the believer to hope without triumphalism. The victory that is certain is the final triumph of grace over the noxious powers of this world, not one's personal seat at the heavenly banquet.

Aquinas, in short, is speaking of what he sees as the general, irreversible tendency of post-resurrection history, not of the destiny of any particular individual. As far as that goes, this general assurance must be laced with doubt and anxiety, since no one can be a free agent and still be assured of his or her salvation. It may be that there is plenty of love and mercy, but not for us. For both the presumptuous and the progressivist, one can be saved without having to stir oneself overmuch, since a felicitous outcome is inscribed in the laws of history. Paul, by contrast, may preach that hope can never delude, but he also insists that salvation must be worked for. For the Council of Trent, presumption means to number oneself among the saved with absolute, infallible certainty, an arrogance or *perversa securitas* (in Augustine's phrase) that is likely to breed spiritual lethargy. No doubt this is why Augustine remarks in his commentary on the Psalms that hope is given only to the humble. Hope for Christian belief is grounded in God's love and mercy, and these are indeed seen as certain. They belong to what it is for God to be God. In this sense, Christianity is a far more deterministic creed than Marxism, a point lost on those religious conservatives who scoff at Marxism for being supposedly committed to cast-iron historical laws. Not only is the reign of God bound to arrive, but it has already done so in principle in the resurrection of Jesus, and humankind is accordingly living in the last days. The fact that all is fundamentally well with history, however, does not entail that all is fundamentally well with any particular participant in it, or that the Wall Street wolves will lie down with the lambs.

Josef Pieper, who regards presumption as a 'fraudulent imitation' of hope, sees it as failing to recognise the arduous nature of constructing a future. As with the Marxist determinists and bourgeois progressivists, the future for those who presume is already firmly secured. Once the spiritual elect have been saved, there can be no more world-historical development. Everything that matters has happened already, in contrast to the Marxist view that everything that has taken place so far is mere 'pre-history', a grim prolegomenon to history proper. In this sense, presumption is not far removed from despair, which similarly eliminates the possibility of change. As Pieper puts it, the despairing see only divine justice, while the presumptuous look only to divine mercy.

Both are forms of premature foreclosure, freezing history into an immutable fate. Theologically speaking, despair sets aside the fact that the kingdom is bound to come, whereas presumption forgets that it will not arrive without the labour of free human agents. In their different ways, both viewpoints relax the tension between the given and the created.

⁓⁂⁓

There is a sense in which hope is performative as well as optative. The same can be true of desire, which may strive to bring about its own fulfilment. To have confidence in a particular future may help to usher it in, rather as those who look genially about them for friends are more likely to find them than the churlish and curmudgeonly. Ernst Bloch regards such performative hope to be true of political revolution, but it may also be apparent in more mundane matters. Those who doubt they will recover from a grave illness are probably more likely to succumb to it than those who do not. Not to behave as though there is hope may be to ensure that there isn't. On this view, hope is not simply an anticipation of the future but an active force in its constitution. As Shelley writes in *Prometheus Unbound*, 'to hope till Hope creates/ From its own wreck the thing it contemplates'. The lines combine a tragic view of hope with a performative one.

Aquinas, for whom hope does not simply anticipate some future good but struggles to attain it, holds that hope can help you concentrate on overcoming a problem, and by virtue of its agreeable quality can make for more effective action. The same pleasant quality can also help you to persist in a project, with the result that hope, like fear, can become self-fulfilling. Immanuel Kant, who believes that nobody can be righteous without hoping for a reward, also regards hope as a powerful motive for virtuous action. In his view, to hope for the supreme good is to be obliged to exercise all one's powers to bring it about. A modern thinker on the topic, for whom hope is an 'active commitment to the desirability and realisability of a certain end', regards it as an activity rather than a state of mind.[94]

It is not, to be sure, that hope is a self-fulfilling prophecy by which you realise your goal simply by virtue of desiring it. For Aquinas, this would diminish its difficulty. The popular American belief that if you hope hard enough you will achieve what you want belongs to an ideological heritage of voluntarism and idealism, one centred on the indomitable will. For the sake of a rhyme, the American song 'High Hopes' juxtaposes the phrase 'high hopes' with 'high apple pie in the sky hopes', which unwittingly gives the game away, since science has so far been unable to confirm the existence of the latter phenomenon. Even so, the mere act of being able to imagine an alternative future may distance and relativise the present, loosening its grip upon us to the point where the future in question becomes more feasible. This is one reason why the Romantic imagination has a link to radical politics. True hopelessness would be when such imaginings were inconceivable.

It may be, however, that true contentment lies in sheer hopelessness. Such hopelessness need not mean despair. On the contrary, it may prove the most potent curative for it. The teaching of the Stoics is that those who do not soar too high cannot be cast down. It is a message to be found as late as the fiction of Thomas Hardy. A number of Hardy's characters come to grief because they aspire unrealistically, while others do so because they are too quick to view their situations as irreparable. It is always imprudent in Hardy to absolutise one's own perspective. There may always be a viewpoint from which some felicity invisible from where you are standing can be glimpsed. In this sense, the fact that the world is fragmentary and conflictive is a source of hope. It is better to live ironically, acknowledging how what might seem momentous to you is mere backdrop to the existence of someone else. Not to hope unfeasibly is to store against one's ruin. The opposite of hope may not be despair but a courageous spirit of resignation. Spinoza, who describes hope in his *Ethics* as 'unsteady joy' (unsteady because uncertain), set his face against both hope and fear. The rational individual lives by assured knowledge, while hope is the illusion of the ignorant.

'The truth is', writes an English journalist who served twenty years of a life sentence in prison, 'that hope for a lifer is exhausting. It stops you sleeping and can drive you insane - much safer to expect nothing and never to be disappointed.'[95] 'One salvation remains to the defeated - to hope for none', reads a line of Virgil's *Aeneid*. No one is more insulated from illusion than those who have been thoroughly crushed. Ataraxy, or tranquility of mind, is best preserved by foreclosing future possibility. To ensure that one's victories are minor is to warrant that one's failures are equally modest. If the good life is one of placid self-possession, it is necessary to abandon both hope and despair, moods that render us prey to the ravages of time. To jettison the future is an instant cure for anxiety. Plato's *Republic* sees the contented soul as one immune to shifts of fortune, resting placidly in itself rather than risking attachment to others. Aristotle, by contrast, argues in both the *Ethics* and the *Politics* that a life without risk and vulnerability is an impoverished one. Cicero writes of those fortunate souls who are 'alarmed by no fears, anguished by no distresses, disturbed by no cravings, dissolved into no voluptuous languors by fatuous transports of delight'.[96] In *The Myth of Sisyphus*, Albert Camus admonishes us to abandon hope, at least of the religious kind.

For the Stoics, the most gratifying solution to the indignities of life is death; but this goal can always be prefigured in the present in the living death or cultivated impassivity of those who lay violent hands upon themselves, rendering themselves immune to both desire and disenchantment. 'Where there's death, there's hope', remarks Don Fabrizio in Tomasi di Lampedusa's *The Leopard*. If it is the catchword of the Stoic, it could also be the motto of the martyr. To be virtuous for the Stoic is not to educate one's appetites but to surmount them. The point of life is not to court Fortune but to disdain it. It is the antithesis of the tragic vision, for which it is the enterprising and ambitious who are most likely to take a tumble. ' 'Tis ever a curse for a man to be marked above the common lot', comment the Chorus in Sophocles' *Philoctetes.* To risk nothing, by contrast, is to lose nothing. One should 'abide in a peaceful state', writes Seneca, 'being never uplifted nor ever cast down'.[97] *Apatheia* is all. The price of serenity is a certain redemptive monotony. The Stoic is present and absent in the world at the same time, both living and dead, pitched into its turbulent affairs yet quarantined from its vicissitudes by his nobility of soul. Those who hope are present and absent in a different sense, divided as they are between what is palpable but imperfect and what is absent but alluring, between the insistence of the actual and the promise of a future. Schopenhauer regards hope as the root of evil, disturbing one's tranquility with false expectations. 'Every wish soon dies', he writes, 'and so can beget no more pain [i.e., of disappointment], if no hope nourishes it.'[98] For Theodore Hickey of Eugene O'Neill's *The Iceman Cometh*, to abandon hope means that 'you can let go of yourself at last. Let yourself sink down to the bottom of the sea. Rest in peace. There's no further you have to go. Not a single damned hope or dream left to nag you' (act 2). It is not a view that proves particularly fruitful for the bums and barflies around him, or in the end for himself.

An alternative way of avoiding the lures of false hope is not to suppress one's desires but to gratify them. If one could live permanently at the point of perfect fulfilment, one would be free of all lack, therefore of all hope, and consequently of all disappointment. This is the last-ditch strategy of Shakespeare's Antony and Cleopatra, who by cramming every moment to the full seek to outwit aspiration by outflanking time. (A rather more cavalier version of the project can be found in some of John Donne's love poems.) The opening lines of the play speak of Antony as 'o'erflow[ing] the measure', like a fountain that brims over but constantly renews itself. Yeats presents us with such an icon in the first stanza of 'Meditations in Time of Civil War':

Surely among a rich man's flowering lawns,
Amid the rustle of his planted hills,
Life overflows without ambitious pains,
And rains down life until the basin spills,
And mounts more dizzy high the more it rains
As though to choose what shape it wills,
And never stoop to a mechanical
Or servile shape, at others' beck and call.

The image is one of perpetual surfeit and replenishment. In a similar way, according to Antony, 'The higher Nilus swells,/The more it promises' (act 2, scene 7). Cleopatra speaks of her lover's bounty as 'an autumn . . ./That grew the more by reaping' (act 5, scene 2). There is no deficit here, and hence no desire. According to Enobarbus, Cleopatra 'makes hungry/Where most she satisfies' (act 2, scene 2), meaning that desire is simply one moment of repletion en route to another. Fullness breeds yet more fullness, in a condition that in 'Credences of Summer' Wallace Stevens calls 'the barrenness/Of the fertile thing that can attain no more'.

One might say of the play's lovers what Florizel says of Perdita in *The Winter's Tale*: 'Each your doing,/So singular in each particular,/Crowns what you are doing in the present deeds,/That all your acts are queens' (act 4, scene 4). Or as Octavius rather more disdainfully puts it, Antony fills 'his vacancy with his voluptuousness', 'pawning [his] experience to [his] present pleasure' and thus obliterating his past (act 1, scene 4). What seems to the play's eponymous characters a blessed release from the burden of history is in the buttoned-downed Octavius's view a form of stagnant self-consuming. The fickle-minded common people, he declares, 'Like to a vagabond flag [reed] upon the stream,/Goes to and back, lackeying the varying tide,/To rot itself with motion' (act 1, scene 4), but the description could equally apply to his view of Antony and Cleopatra. Octavius is not an admirer of those energetically intent on getting nowhere.

For the play's lovers, each moment of time, being packed full of delectation, becomes absolute, and thus figures as an image of eternity. To live as intensely as this is to transcend death and decay, and thus to be hopeless in the sense of having no need of the virtue. Expectation is annulled along with futurity. In another sense, to live in this way is to prefigure the eternity that death will usher in, as one seeks to position oneself in the present at the still point of the end of time, and by anticipating the consummation of death in the *pleroma* of the present, disarm it of its terrors. So it is that Antony, pleasurably at ease in the grip of Thanatos or the death drive, speaks of running toward his death with all the erotic eagerness of a bridegroom to the bridal bed. Since each moment of time is self-contained, there can be no sequencing or subordination of one to the other, and thus no question of project, causality, aspiration, anticipation and their attendant frustrations. 'My powers are crescent, and my auguring hope / Says it will come to the full' (act 2, scene 1), boasts Pompey; but talk of growth, hope, foresight and expectation in this play is the discourse of Rome, not the idiom of Egypt. Since the time of sensuous pleasure is not the time of human agency, history in Alexandria is abolished, except when it taps on Antony's shoulder in the form of a summons to the imperial metropolis. The subject of pleasure is one absolved from historical change and temporal sequence ('Eternity was in our lips and eyes'), rather as the figures of Antony and Cleopatra themselves, being legendary creatures in the eyes of Shakespeare's audience, loom up as monuments of a timeless present.

3

The Philosopher of Hope

ERNST BLOCH IS *the* philosopher of hope, rather as Nietzsche is without question the philosopher of power and Heidegger beyond doubt the philosopher of Being. One of the great luminaries of Western Marxism, he is also among the most neglected of that band, a neglect that may not be unrelated to the fact that his magnum opus, *The Principle of Hope*, runs to almost 1,400 pages in English translation. The eager expectancy of an end, an attitude that the book portrays in utopian terms, can thus be a familiar experience for some of its readers as well. Even Perry Anderson, whose erudition would appear to match Bloch's own, omits all mention of him in his classic *Considerations on Western Marxism*.

Matters are not helped by the turgid, oracular prose in which some of Bloch's work is cast. Jürgen Habermas, who describes his style as 'late Expressionist', comments that 'there are erratic blocks of hyphenated terminology, luxuriant growths of pleonastic tropes, the heaving of dithyrambic breath'.[1] There are also formulations that do not exactly trip off the tongue, as when he writes (in a sentence chosen almost at random) of 'the overbright consternation of the astonishment at flashing moments and signatures of adequation in the bed-chamber of the lived moment'.[2] Despite some passages of burnished splendour, Bloch's overstuffed rhetoric, slipshod poeticisms, and pseudoprofundities are the kind of thing that gives Marxist theory a bad name.

If his style prefigures utopia in its imaginative brio, it also does so in its obscurity. Rarely has St Paul's remark about seeing the kingdom of God through a glass darkly been more apposite. One turns with relief from Bloch's rhapsodic prose to the terse, aphoristic economy of Benjamin or Adorno.

The form of Bloch's major study reflects its content. This great grab-bag of a book disowns any rigorous structure in the name of freedom and diversity, values that foreshadow the future of which it speaks. The very act of reading it is thus meant to give us a taste of utopia. Centralised planning and hierarchical ordering are set aside, as they will be in the realm of communism. Whereas the Stalinist conception of totality rides roughshod over the specific, Bloch's wayward, idiosyncratic imagination does full justice to the random and contingent, as one richly detailed digression follows hard on the heels of another. The strange materialist poetry of his work, along with its refusal of conventional design, is a political gesture in itself, representing as it does a sustained assault on the protocols of orthodox scholarship. Theodor Adorno speaks of his offences against the 'ceremonials of intellectual discipline'.[3]

As a left-wing German Jew, Bloch spent the Nazi years in various European refuges and in 1938 migrated to the United States, which is where *The Principle of Hope* was written. He moved to East Germany in 1949, where, as one commentator remarks, 'for the sake of the future he made a Faustian pact with the duplicitous present'.[4] He became, in short, a full-blooded apologist for Stalinism, defending the Moscow show trials and branding Trotsky a Gestapo agent. Though he kept his distance from the Communist Party, he indulged on occasions in the crudest Stalinist polemics, repeatedly professing his absolute loyalty to the East German regime. As Habermas puts it, Bloch had no doubt that the road to freedom and plurality led through state power, violence, centralised planning, collectivism and doctrinal orthodoxy.[5] Like many of his colleagues on the left, he saw the key choice of the era as one between Stalin and Hitler. Even so, to glimpse the seeds of utopia in the Soviet Union represented a signal triumph of hope over experience, rather as writing about hope in the German Democratic Republic was a remarkable victory over the experience of living there.

Despite Bloch's faith in the GDR, a wild farrago of mysticism and metaphysics, which is how the regime viewed *The Principle of Hope*, was unlikely to endear him to the authorities there. If Marxism could predict the future with scientific precision, what need was there for a petty-bourgeois piety like hope? Bloch was accordingly hounded, reviled and banned from teaching and publishing. Prevented from returning home on a visit to West Berlin in 1961 by the rise of the Berlin Wall, he decided to remain on the Western side of the divide, where he turned furiously on his former Stalinist masters. To his credit, he refused to tread the familiar path of disenchanted leftist turned strident reactionary. Instead, he lent his support to the student, anti-nuclear and anti-Vietnam War movements, castigating the German ruling class where he saw fit. He was to end up as one of the most revered prophets of the Western Left, a mythological figure even in his own lifetime.

Perry Anderson has noted that an openness to non-Marxist thought is a distinctive feature of Western Marxism, from the influence of Croce on Gramsci and Hegel on Adorno to Heidegger on Sartre and Spinoza on Althusser.[6] One might claim that Bloch's writings press this receptiveness to a parodic extreme. His dauntingly encyclopaedic knowledge extends to what Habermas (who finds Bloch's lack of conceptual precision 'obnoxious') calls 'Pythagorean number symbolism, Cabbalistic teaching on signatures, hermetic physiognomies, alchemy and astrology'.[7] It was not quite the daily fare of the East Berlin bureaucrats. In his early work *The Spirit of Utopia*, Bloch had combined Jewish Messianism and classical philosophy, occultism and eschatology, Marxism and theosophy. The sheer spaciousness of his writings is breathtaking. Leszek Kołakowski speaks of his attempt to graft 'a complete metaphysic, cosmology, and speculative cosmogony' onto Marxism.[8]

The Principle of Hope is in search of a form of Marxism that would rival the depth and scope of religion while serving as a critique of it. It ranges accordingly from the Gnostics to the modernists, Boehme to Bolshevism, Eldorado to Joachim de Fiore, the Orinoco delta to roast pigeons and Aladdin's lamp. Its author's interests stretch from ethics, aesthetics, mythology, natural law and anthropology to fantasy, popular culture, sexuality, religion and the natural environment. He also inveighs against the Eurocentric bias of classical Marxism, insisting on the need to give full weight to non-European cultures. No other historical materialist, write two of his commentators, 'has more convincingly demonstrated the importance of philosophy, art, and religion for revolutionary practice'.[9] In this respect, he is the kind of Marxist with whom critics of Marxism may feel at home. It is no surprise, then, that he has been assiduously courted by liberation theologians, cultural historians, liberal humanists and a range of others generously prepared to overlook his unswerving devotion to the dialectics of matter.

As one who railed against what he called 'the malnutrition of the socialist imagination', however, Bloch is at risk of a conceptual obesity of Rabelaisian proportions. What some might see as impressive erudition, others might regard as an alarming case of intellectual bulimia. Nothing could be further from his overblown sensibility than the classical virtues of tact and reticence. The very ideas of sparseness and obliquity are unknown to him. His thought is powered by a well-nigh pathological drive for universal knowledge, one that prefigures the so-called *Totum* of communist utopia. In this sense, too, the form of his work is at one with its content. Yet the paradox of this stunningly diverse body of work is its fundamentally monotone quality. Its prodigal range exemplifies again and again the same rather slender set of concerns. The remarkable richness of Bloch's writing is more empirical than conceptual, as a relatively small cluster of key notions, many of them more or less synonymous with one another, are illustrated by an extraordinary expanse of concrete phenomena. The repetitiveness of his writing is astonishing. *Totum* and *Ultimum* are also *Optimum* and *summum bonum*, while *Heimat*,

Being, the All, *eschaton* and *pleroma* are more or less interchange-able. Apart from the fact that all these terms gesture to a future state of peace, freedom and classlessness, they are notably low on content.

One might claim that Bloch's writing is at once too little Marx-ist and too much so - too eager to assume that almost every his-torical phenomenon, however remote from modern politics, can be milked for its emancipatory value, yet too intent on funnelling this prodigious mass of material into the mold of historical ma-terialism. The past may be diverse, but it has a single destina-tion. So it is that Bloch the Stalinist exists cheek by jowl with Bloch the snapper-up of unconsidered trifles, the apologist for the heretical and offbeat, scouring the crooked alleyways and in-conspicuous backstreets of human culture. If his vision is too dif-fuse, it is also too constricted. His work amplifies and diminishes at the same time. It is crammed with a profuse variety of odds and ends, but also represents the mother of all metanarratives. There is too much loose talk about cosmic forces, but also too much schematic stuff about the dialectics of matter. *The Principle of Hope* is hospitable to the whole wealth of human culture - but only in the end in order to appropriate it. Marxism is the legatee of all previous creative thought, but trumps it in the act of tak-ing it over. There are times, for example, when Bloch seems to suggest that almost all pre-Marxist thought is unschooled in the future tense. Futurity is born along with historical materialism. As the concrete realisation of the kernel of truth to be found in all earlier visions of freedom, Marx's thought brings to fruition a legacy passed down from the Hebrew prophets and Paracel-sus to Hegel and the modern age. Is finding evidence of proto-Marxism everywhere one looks a question of being open-minded or tunnel-visioned?

If Bloch is a standard Western Marxist in his stance to non-Marxist thought, he is untypical of the school in his affirmative spirit. Perry Anderson points out in his survey of Western Marx-ism that a vein of melancholy runs through several of its thinkers, whereas Bloch might reasonably be accused of excessive cheerfulness. There may be historical reasons for this sanguine vista. If hope in Bloch's view is an ontological affair rather than a state of mind, it is perhaps because only an assurance as deep-seated as this could survive the dark historical age through which he lived. Common-or-garden hope might not have proved resilient enough. To affirm so robustly in such desolate times demands either an uncommon amount of vision or an unusual degree of blindness. Perhaps the hope at stake here is one that no mere empirical defeat could rebuff. Is Bloch's brand of hope indefeasible because it is without reason?[10]

Bloch certainly writes as though hope is built into the structure of the world itself. In this resolute ontologising of the virtue, there is hope in the world almost as there is uranium. Intention, expectation and anticipation are less aspects of consciousness than fundamental determinants of reality itself. There is a 'good which is working its way through',[11] or as a character in Beckett's *Endgame* remarks rather more ominously, 'Something is taking its course.' It is as though Being itself is hope in its very essence, such that without this inner striving it would lapse into nothingness. 'The substance-formations of the world', Bloch claims, '. . . are full of the tendency of the Not-Yet towards the All.'[12] Future possibility, he believes, must be 'objectively-real' rather than purely subjective, latent in the present situation rather than mere wishful thinking. This, as we have seen, is also true of Marx, but Bloch presses the matter a stage or two further. It is not just that one must have material grounds for hope, but that hope for Bloch is in some sense an objective dynamic in the world - not only in human history, indeed, but in the cosmos itself. He is intent, he tells us, on producing nothing less than a communist cosmology. Marx, by contrast, may trust to the evolution of the productive forces, but he does not claim that this unfolding is somehow inscribed in the stuff of the world. It is not a metaphysical principle, as with Hegel's *Geist* or Bergson's *élan vital*. Instead, it is confined to the historical arena. Marx is impatient with metaphysical speculation, and appears to take no interest in how the cosmos is faring. He does not claim that the world itself is trekking toward a beneficent end. Bloch speaks of 'the classless man' as representing 'the ultimately intended propensity-possibility of history up to now',[13] but Marx indulges in no such transhistorical fantasies. Indeed, he is at pains to deny that history has purposes of its own. Nor does he argue for some tale of unbroken progress at the moral level, as we have noted already. Fascism is no advance on feudalism.

It may be true that reality is constantly evolving, but this would be a reason for hope only if change were desirable in itself. As a Romantic vitalist, Bloch is often to be found writing as though motion, dynamism, mutability, transience, instability, productivity, open-endedness, possibility and the like are unequivocally positive, which is clearly not the case. 'Mobile, changing, changeable Being', he asserts, '. . . has the unclosed capability of becoming.'[14] He does not add that some of its potential futures might turn out to be thoroughly unpleasant. Futurity is not a value in itself, apart perhaps for Wall Street speculators. One should not rejoice at the mere prospect of open-endedness. The Third Reich rejected closure, intent as it was on enduring indefinitely. No historical system has been more mutable than capitalism, as the *Communist Manifesto* is keen to point out. Genocide is a dynamic process. To unfurl is not necessarily to flourish. Things can become tarnished in the act of unfolding, as well as becoming more fully themselves. The conservative suspects that this is true as a general rule, and that the only commendable form of change is therefore one that seeks to preserve the status quo. He or she has hopes for the future, but only in the sense that it will be more or less continuous with the present. This need not imply complacency about the status quo, simply a reluctance to jeopardise it by taking a leap into the unknown.

It is not only Platonists who regard mutability as a mark of imperfection. As a Messianic thinker, Walter Benjamin saw the transience of history as bound up with its negligibility. It is also worth noting that there is also nothing inherently objectionable about stasis. Changelessness can be an admirable condition. One trusts that granting of the vote to women will not turn out to be a passing fad, and that the laws prohibiting child labour do not disappear from the statute book. Change is positive only when measured by certain moral criteria, not as viewed from the standpoint of the universe itself; and Bloch faces the familiar historicist problem of knowing from where these criteria are to be derived, and how they can stand in judgment on a history of which they are part. Perhaps historical phenomena are to be assessed in terms of how far they contribute to the emergence of the All or *Totum* of the future; but since this *telos* has not yet arrived - since history does not yet constitute a totality - it is hard to know how one can appeal to it as a yardstick by which to judge the process that will bring it to birth.

It is equally hard to know what sense to make of the claim that hope is inherent in material process. In one sense, it seems as absurd as insisting that envy or ambition is also an intrinsic feature of it. For Bloch, as Wayne Hudson puts it, 'It is reality, and not merely consciousness, which has futuristic properties.'[15] It is true that reality has futuristic properties in the sense that it evolves, but this is not to say that the evolution is directed to a laudable end. Even if there is a dynamic at the heart of matter urging it onward, it does not follow that it is also propelling it upward. Only if one regards change as productive in itself would this be so. That they may last for a century or so, or be confined to certain regions of West Africa, may be properties of historical phenomena, but not that they are pregnant with a state of bliss. The cosmos is no more intent on improvement than it is hell-bent on self-destruction. The Victorian philosopher Herbert Spencer taught that the world becomes increasingly heterogeneous as it evolves; but this only constitutes grounds for hope if one regards heterogeneity as a condition to be commended, which is a matter of opinion. The same applies to claims that the world is growing more unified, or that civilisation is en route to producing higher intelligence, healthier babies, and increasing longevity. That babies should be born cleverer, healthier or prettier is no cause for celebration for those who regard human existence as pointless in the first place. Those who abhor the idea of communism would not regard Bloch's future as worth hoping for.

The whole of material reality, Bloch believes, is pervaded by an inherent purposiveness or tendency to perfection. How he knows this is hard to say. It would seem just the kind of speculative viewpoint he himself scorns when it crops up in the guise of bourgeois idealism. In fact, it sounds uncomfortably close to bourgeois ideology at its most crassly triumphalist. In this mood, Bloch sounds more like Teihard de Chardin than a disciple of Marx. He also echoes the thought of a radical like Georg Büchner, who despite the unmitigated bleakness of his drama held that Nature was powered by a law that made for unity and harmony. Bloch's vision of progress, as Hudson suggests, springs from replacing God with dialectical matter.[16] In fact, he is one of the few Western Marxists to admire Engels' *Dialectics of Nature*. If matter can oust the Almighty, however, it is because Bloch has smuggled certain quasidivine properties into it from the outset. And if matter replaces God, so in the fullness of time will humanity. Yahweh's promise to his people, for Bloch as for John Milton, is that he will eventually stand down. He will abdicate his throne, surrendering his divine authority to Man in the figure of his Son. Indeed, humanity will not only reign supreme in God's vacated seat but actually surpass him in sovereign power. It is hard to know whether this is an atheistic vision or a religious one.

Dubbed a Marxist Schelling by Habermas, Bloch would seem to posit a creative potential secreted in the very stuff of the cosmos. A theory that for Aristotle applies purely to biological forms is inflated to a whole cosmology. It is less that humanity fosters hope than that it activates resources which are already latent in being. In the grandest of all possible narratives, the same animating impulse is seen to lurk within the most diverse phenomena. There is a sense in which this is a necessary conceptual move. If the various processes that constitute the world are all moving onward and upward, then either this must be a remarkable coincidence, or it must stem from the fact they spring from the same root. Some sort of monism and essentialism must under-lie the doctrine of universal progress, however varied the forms it assumes. Otherwise one could not speak of the world itself as advancing, as opposed to this or that sector of it. One might imagine instead that there is a multiplicity of Not-Yets rather than just one, and that some currents of the cosmos are en route to perfection while others are not.

Given the diversity of those currents, what they share must be some lowest common denominator or utterly rudimentary prin-ciple, which is why Bloch turns for the source of utopia to the basic building blocks of the universe. Yet it is not obvious what it means to say that reality itself reveals a trajectory, or to grasp how communism is implicit in the structure of the amoeba. How could the world itself, as opposed to this or that historical cur-rent within it, be maturing? In what sense is a photon oriented to paradise, to use one of Bloch's own terms for the cosmic end point? However else one judges this mystical materialism, it has little or nothing to do with Marxism. Materialism for Marx is not a metaphysical claim about the nature of matter, but a belief in the primacy of material practice in human affairs.

Bloch does not deny the fact of human depravity. Indeed, in the wake of Auschwitz he calls in Kantian style for a postulate of radical evil. Nor does he claim that the utopian proclivities of the cosmos will necessarily prevail. To do so would be to sail embarrassingly close to the deterministic Marxism he rejects. There is an impulse to self-fulfilment in the world, but it will come to fruition only through free human activity. Otherwise the entire project could easily go awry. The cosmos requires our cooperation. In rising to self-consciousness in humanity, its inner dynamic is actively promoted. Hope is built into the universe, but is in no sense guaranteed and can always be derailed. In this way, Bloch manages to combine a full-blooded teleology with a belief in free will. Indeed, his case is not far from the Christian doctrine of Providence, which holds that the kingdom of heaven is destined to arrive - in fact, that the whole of Creation is even now groaning and travailing toward this end - but that it is part of God's design that men and women, being the recipients of his grace, will freely cooperate with this project.

For Christian faith, as we have seen already, God has ordered the human narrative to a good end, one that cannot come to grief. No historical event, not even a nuclear holocaust or eco-logical catastrophe, can shipwreck the fact that history for the Gospel lies in the embrace of the resurrection. Because of the risen Christ, hope, so to speak, has already happened. The future has already been secured by the past. For Christians, then, hope is indeed in some sense built into the stuff of the cosmos. Christ is the Lord of Creation as well as of history. Yet it is hard to see how the same can be true for Bloch. There is simply nothing in his atheism to warrant it.

If Bloch's view is valid, then it follows that hope flows with the tide of the universe rather than moving against the current. Yet if this is true, any particular act of hope is subtly devalued. Because it partakes in the general tendency of the cosmos, it is a less arduous affair than hope *despite* - hope that refuses to give way even in the most joyless of situations. Rather as Milton is unable to praise a cloistered virtue that feels no need to struggle for its sanctity, so we may find ourselves unimpressed by the kind of hope that comes too easily. Hope does not require the back-ing of the universe, and may be all the more creditable when it dispenses with it. Walter Benjamin regarded the belief that his-tory was on our side as the last word in politically suicidal com-placency. Thomas Hardy, similarly, saw the faith that the uni-verse was in cahoots with humanity as a dangerous sentimental illusion, which is not to say that he thought that the world was working malevolently against us. The universe is not some kind of agent. It is rather that Hardy took the view that reality has no moods or opinions of its own, and that this can be a source of hope as much as a cause for dejection.[17] If the world does not collaborate with our more praiseworthy projects, neither does it conspire with our less reputable ones.

If history reveals a built-in trajectory to utopia, how can this inclination come to grief, as a brief glance around the globe suggcsts might be the case? The answer for *The Principle of Hope* is that it can be thwarted by human activity. The force that drives the world forward is benign in itself, but can always be betrayed. It is humanity, maker and slayer of worlds, which can choose whether to bring the universe to perfection or destruction. In Bloch's view, there is no middle way between the two, though he does not explain why. What is at stake here is an expression/ blockage model of human desire. 'What can become of Man', Bloch inquires, 'if his progress is not blocked?'[18] Left to itself, it would seem, humanity will journey toward the felicity the cosmos has in store for it. The obstacles that might obstruct this progress, for Bloch as for most Romantic libertarians, are external rather than built-in. And since external impediments are for the most part more easily surmounted than internal ones, this itself is a potent source of comfort.

But the model is surely misleading. For one thing, it cannot accommodate the reality of evil, in the sense of an obscene revelling in destruction as an end in itself.[19] It is nonplussed by the kind of nihilism for which human value is purely bogus. For another thing, not all negativity springs from suppressing one's finer instincts. There are other sources of moral damage. Human desires do not grow morbid simply by virtue of being stymied, as the surrealists tended to claim, and as a superficial reading of William Blake might suggest. On the contrary, there are desires which must be suppressed in the name of the general well-being. Romantic libertarianism, however, throws no light on how we are to discriminate between the more and less enlightened of our yearnings.

To realise one's inner being involves not just breaking ecstatically through a set of external barriers, but the rather more exacting business of emancipating ourselves from ourselves. We need to reeducate our desires, not just externalise them freely. As one averse to psychoanalytic theory, Bloch would be unsettled by the suggestion that there is that at the heart of desire that seeks its own negation. Whereas desire for Freud is always in some sense botched and perverse, Bloch treats it in the form of hope as unequivocally positive. Negativity is largely a question of hindrance. It is no part of hope or desire themselves. What curbs our aspirations lies for the most part in the political domain, not, as for Freud, in some censorious Law installed in the very innards of the human subject. Desire for Freud is not some primordial force which runs up against the Law, but the bruising effect of our encounter with it. For his part, Bloch tends to underplay the lack involved in desire for the *promesse de bonheur* it brings with it. He also assumes that its transgressive nature is always on the side of progress. There is little concept of hubris in his hymn to the infinite.

It might be claimed that Marx, too, draws on the expression/repression model, not least in his account of how the productive forces are thwarted by the prevailing social relations. If those forces include humanity itself, as Marx seems to assume, it is easy to imagine that the realisation of human powers is a good in itself, and that the only problem lies in their obstruction. As with most exponents of an ethics of self-realisation, Marx needs to be more alert than he is to the problem of how we are to distinguish among our capabilities, some of which are a good deal more injurious than others. Otherwise he is in danger of assuming in naively libertarian style that the very existence of a capability is sufficient grounds for its realisation.

Marx's overall view of history, however, is not so simplistic. For one thing, communism is the product of political revolution, not of the cosmos. For another thing, the claim that he views the evolution of the productive forces as constituting a metanarrative has been vigorously contested.[20] In any case, we have seen already that the unleashing of these forces will prove beneficial only in the long run. In the shorter term, it generates barbarism as well as civilisation. History, like Tristram Shandy's doomed autobiography, is thus progressive and regressive at the same time. If it forges ahead, it does so, Marx insists, by its bad side. The resources bequeathed by the past to the present are tainted goods, poisoned gifts, as both Marx and Freud are aware. Besides, though one might read Marx as positing a certain continuity of evolution in the material base, he makes no such claims for the so-called superstructure; whereas there is a sense in which for Bloch the superstructure, too, represents a formidable grand narrative, as its art, culture, politics and religion can be grasped as so many diverse expressions of the same underlying principle of hope.

If you reduce hope to a single positive force, it is hard to account for the kind of aspirations that are noxious through and through. Hoping to eliminate the Jews from Europe or the kulaks from Soviet Russia are cases in point. It is not that Bloch entirely ignores such malign projects, but that he is insufficiently disturbed by them. The term 'hope' has too buoyant a resonance for him to confront them squarely. In fact, he can detect a utopian impulse, however monstrously deformed, in even the most malevolent of aspirations.

There are some benefits to be reaped from this viewpoint. It allows him, for example, to take a far more nuanced view of fascism than those Marxists of his day for whom it represented no more than the death throes of capitalism, and was thus in some sense to be welcomed. Bloch, who investigates forms of popular consciousness and calls for a new *Kulturpolitik*, takes what Marxism terms the cultural superstructure with admirable seriousness, discerning in the myths and fantasies of fascism, for example, certain warped desires which might otherwise have proved politically fruitful. As Fredric Jameson puts it, he clings to the 'underlying principle that every negative in some fashion implies a positive which is ontologically prior to it'.[21] Or as Jürgen Habermas remarks in similar vein, 'He wants to save what is true in false consciousness.'[22]

All the same, there are limits to this generosity of spirit. It is not true that every dreamer is a closet revolutionary. To detect a positive impulse, however grossly disfigured, in the wish to cleanse the world of Jews would count as a moral obscenity. Not all hope is a foretaste of utopia. The unity of a lynch mob is not best seen as a distorted premonition of the communist future. There are ways of transforming the world that do not testify to the utopian spirit. Murder, for example, implies a faith in the possibility of change, the provisional nature of the present, and the open-ended character of history. It cannot be the case, then, that, as Fredric Jameson writes, 'wherever we look everything in the world becomes a version of some primal figure, a manifestation of that primordial movement toward the future . . . which is utopia'.[23] To see hope and its goal as singular, however - to hold that all human hopes are secretly one, and that all of them strive for the same emancipated future - is to court just such an error.

Besides, to wrench the whole world so firmly round on its axis to face the future, so that all authentic thought becomes anticipatory, all genuine art utopian, and all valid action a foretaste of the Not-Yet, is to diminish the actual in the act of dignifying it. It is to lend art, thought and action a momentous significance while claiming that their truth lies outside themselves. Reality is absented from itself, perpetually deferred to some speculative *telos*. 'Only the horizon of the future, which Marxism occupies, with that of the past as an ante-room, gives reality its real dimension', Bloch asserts.[24] The world as it exists, he comments, is 'not true'. But neither is such a claim. It is not the case that what has still to achieve its full potential is thereby deficient in reality. An egg is not defective because it is not yet a chicken, or a programme of political reform vacuous because it falls short of utopia. The present is not ontologically inferior to the future. Nor is the past a mere prelude to the present. The subjunctive should not be allowed to trump the indicative. Ludwig Wittgenstein warns in his *Philosophical Investigations* against arguing that there is no last house in the village because we could always build another one. So we could; but that does not alter the fact that there is a last house here and now. The village can be extended, for sure, but it is not unfinished.

One of the most disreputable aspects of Bloch's writing is his contempt for the empirical. Kołakowski writes acidly of how he raises an incapacity for analysis to the rank of a theoretical virtue.[25] There are times when he sails perilously close to the vulgar-Romantic prejudice that facts are simply reifications, and statements of fact ipso facto 'positivist'. It is thus that he can speak derisively of 'merely factual reality'. Existing states of affairs are simply snapshots of a deeper process, which alone is real. *Vernunft* is superior to *Verstand*, the imagination incomparably more precious than routine rationality. The actual is for those craven souls who cannot stomach the possible. To steep oneself in it too deeply is a form of denial. The utopian vision cannot be refuted by anything as lowbrow as what happens to be the case.

There is a relation between this lofty ontology and Bloch's Stalinism. If only the communist future is truly real, one can put up with the barbarism involved in constructing it. If the cosmos perpetually defers its own *telos*, so too does the East German regime. In this sense, Bloch's Not-Yet is a species of theodicy. It may also be the case that reflections on the *Totum, Ultimum, Ens Perfectissimum,* What-Essence, That-Ground and other such portentous abstractions can help to shield you from the realpolitik of the present. If Bloch keeps the idea of hope alive in what Bertolt Brecht called the new ice age, it is partly, one suspects, because his love affair with the future acts as a defence against the terrors of his time. If those who idolise the present disavow the future, the opposite may also be true.

The kind of hope that Bloch affirms is one we have already dubbed fundamental – hope in an imposing upper case, rather than this or that particular craving. As with Freudian desire, its object is obscure and indeterminate, since its *pleroma* is a currently inconceivable state of affairs. It follows that hope for Bloch is in one sense almost as objective as a blow on the head, yet in another sense exasperatingly elusive. Its fulfilment can be glimpsed in daydreams and fantasies, stray moments of *jouissance* and new styles of architecture; but it cannot be confronted head-on, any more than the Jews were permitted to carve graven images of Yahweh the non-God. For Freud, too, dreams and fantasies constitute a kind of symptomatology, but in his case it is the past that they evoke, not the future. Whereas he treats them as signifiers of some primal trauma, Bloch, who regards psychoanalysis as the product of a washed-up bourgeois class, finds in them foretastes of what is to come, somewhat in the way that the sacramental life is for Christianity. He does not seem to recognise that the scene of analysis excavates the past for the sake of an emancipated future. If Bloch is on the trail of the future-in-the-past, so in a different sense is Freud. In the latter's view, the present is constantly dragged back by the undertow of the past, while for Bloch it gains traction through the tidal tug of the future. In both cases, the present moment is pregnant with a momentous kind of otherness. For Freud, the end lies in the origin, as the bruised ego struggles to return to a point before its hapless emergence; for Bloch, in one of his most renowned slogans, the genesis is at the end. The future for Freud is death, and for Bloch, life. Freud's vision is a tragic one, which is not to say that nothing can be done to repair the ravages of desire, whereas Bloch's, as we shall see in a moment, is too little so.

Upper-case hope, as one might call it, turns human history into a mighty metanarrative, but in Bloch's case this is not a smoothly linear process. It is possible to read his work as a spiritualised version of the Second International Marxism he rejected – one that preserves its totalising, teleological forms but invests them with a different principle. If, however, the future really is secretly at work in the present, linear time gives way to a more looped, multilayered, nonsynchronous vision of history – one that so Bloch rightly considered, Marxism stood in urgent need of. In this sense his vision of history is multiple and monistic at the same time. Precisely because everything in this sprawling text springs from the same unfolding principle, you can cut in and out of the storyline, read it both backwards and forwards, juxtapose the remote with the near at hand, draw far-flung phenomena into unity, and find the future buried in the ancient past.[26] If there is a Benjaminesque aspect to this way of seeing, it is one bound up with a more orthodox Marxist outlook. Whereas hope for Benjamin is at odds with historicism, Bloch runs the two together.

There is a sense in which linear history is potentially tragic history, since what is done cannot be undone. There are cyclical theories of the human narrative for which nothing is ever entirely lost – in which everything will eventually return in modified guise, and which are thus comic rather than tragic. Both Yeats and Joyce held such a view. Linear time, by contrast, may allow one to grow, repent, move on, make restitution, but it is also absolute and implacable. Reimagine and reactivate them as we wish, the dead remain dead and the defeated remain crushed. Hence the tragic tenor of Benjamin's Marxism, which is not the case with Bloch's. Indeed, tragedy is at odds with the whole ambience of his thought. He is clear that what comes next is not always an improvement on what has gone before, and that there are what he calls 'losses on the march forward'; but *The Principle of Hope* has scarcely got off the ground before it comes up with the ominous assertion that 'hope is in love with success rather than failure'.[27] Bloch acknowledges the reality of tragedy, but he is not for the most part a tragic thinker – not because he is a utopian visionary, but because he recognises only fitfully that a transformed existence can spring only from an encounter with dispossession.

There are times, to be sure, when he takes the full pressure of this truth. Only by a confrontation with the void can new life emerge. He writes in *The Principle of Hope* of how 'the humanity of Marx, which is turned toward the humblest of his brothers, proves itself by comprehending the humbleness, the resultant nullity of most of his brothers in its foundations, in order to prize them from the foundations. The zero point of extremest alienation which the proletariat represents now at last becomes the dialectical point of change: Marx teaches us to find our All precisely in the Nothing of this zero point.'[28] It is an arresting insight into the tragic nature of Marxism – a tragedy which is by no means undercut by its positive political goals, since a loss of being is a condition of achieving them. If these words of Bloch are remarkable, however, it is not least because they cut against much else in his general sensibility. Such a tragic perception is by no means the keynote of his work. *The Principle of Hope* gives one little sense of immersing itself in the malignant impulses with which hope has to contend. We do not hear as much as we should of the arrogance of power, the stubborn persistence of violence and self-interest in every epoch of human history, the chronic recurrence of internecine conflicts, the prevalence of false consciousness, the deep-seated drive to maim, exploit and humiliate. Any humanism that turns its eyes from such unsavoury realities is bound to buy its hope on the cheap. Past history for Bloch is for the most part a foretaste of paradise, not, as for Marx, a nightmare that weighs on the brains of the living.

What Bloch is more commonly to be found promoting is not tragedy but theodicy. 'Every advent', he writes, 'contains nihilism as something utilised and defeated, death as something devoured in victory.'[29] Failure is alchemised into success, and mortality recuperated as triumph. 'Nothingness, breaking with greater and greater strength into history, has given constitutive power to the dialectic toward the All itself.'[30] Negativity is simply the motor of progress, as the Not-Yet 'drives on ahead in a utopian and dialectical fashion'.[31] It is true that Bloch concedes the possibility of a bleaker kind of Nothing, one which would spell the collapse of the entire historical process, and which no dialectical sleight of hand could assimilate. Short of such catastrophe, however, negativity would seem to imply an opportunity for moral and political muscle-building. Disasters that cannot be rationalised away in this fashion are drastically belittled. 'Annihilations like the Peloponnesian Wars, the Thirty Years' War', Bloch announces astonishingly, 'are merely misfortunes, not dialectical change; the mortification of Nero, Hitler, all these apparently Satanic outbursts belong to the dragon of the final abyss, not the furthering of history.'[32] The Thirty Years' War, it would seem, was a mere misfortune, a historical aberration, a random diversion from the dialectical highway of history. Hitler is simply a Satanic outburst without historical rationale. Whatever fails to promote historical hope is not genuinely historical at all. Bloch thus shows himself blind to one of the most chilling aspects of the so-called Final

Solution, namely that it was a world-historical event on an epic scale, part of a sinister historical logic, which was also entirely futile, sheer waste and senselessness, a negativity which haunts modern history yet with which nothing constructive can be done. As such, it gives the lie to Bloch's manic Hegelianism.

It is sometimes forgotten that in the phrase *Et in Arcadia Ego* (And I am in Paradise), the speaker is Death. No conceivable utopia could overcome the fact of human mortality. With a mixture of hubris and sophistry, however, Bloch, for whom in a more sombre mood death is the ultimate anti-utopia, hints that even this might finally prove possible. There is more than one vague gesture toward immortality in *The Principle of Hope*. 'The certainty of class consciousness', he writes, '. . . is indeed a Novum against death', meaning that though I die, we shall not.[33] Besides, if one's true identity lies in the future, it cannot be destroyed because it does not yet exist. What has not yet come to be cannot pass away. There have been more rigorous arguments in the history of philosophy. A life that has been fully realised, Bloch suggests, cannot be touched by death. Full self-achievement would spell the end of time and process, and mortality along with them. There is an 'immortal element' at the core of each individual, so that 'whenever existence comes near to its core, permanence begins'.[34] In Epicurean phrase: Where Man is, death is not. It is a moving sentiment, if wholly untrue. In fact, the opposite is the case. It is with humanity that death comes to self-consciousness.

Bloch's attitude to death is profoundly un-Marxist, but it is almost equally un-Christian. Christianity does not teach that there is an imperishable spirit at the core of the individual which will survive the wreck of the body. It holds rather that there is no authentic personal identity without the body, which is why redemption must involve its resurrection; and that though death is an outrage, it is only by bowing to its necessity, in an act of self-dispossession which is at the same time the inner structure of love, that its sting can be drawn. The resurrection for Bloch signifies the possibility of immortality, but he does not sufficiently ponder the fact that there can be no resurrection without crucifixion. Death must be lived all the way through if it is to prove fruitful, traversed to its limit rather than disavowed in some fantasy of invulnerability. Only in this way can power be plucked from weakness. Christianity is at one with Marxism in its faith that authentic existence can spring only from a loss of being, and both creeds are at odds in this respect with Blochian triumphalism. Bloch may take Kierkegaard's point in *The Sickness Unto Death* that the redeemable life must pass through every form of negativity, but it is hard to feel that, in Hegelian phrase, he tarries enough with the negative – that hope is capable of submitting itself to its ravages without a single guarantee up its sleeve, or can confront the possibility that the whole human enterprise may be an exercise in sheer absurdity. Hope, to be enduring and well-founded, needs to be dearly bought, whereas one problem with Bloch's universe is that the place is awash with the stuff. It is visible everywhere you look, in this folk tale or that mythological image, this piece of arcane wisdom or that inspiring configuration of space.

In this sense, hope is too pervasively immanent in reality; yet it is also too transcendent, too little of this world. What it finally aims for is perfection. It is an unreasonable end; and those who invite us to hope unreasonably risk plunging us into chronic disaffection. There is an alarming all-or-nothingness about Bloch's reflections, an aversion to settling for half, a quasi-pathological drive for repletion. It can be felt in the avidity with which he absorbs such vast swathes of human culture. The Blochian imagination is excessive, hyperbolic, full to bursting point, as though the faintest hint of deficiency would threaten its dream of perfection. No doubt this is another reason for Bloch's animus against Freud, for whom even gratified desire contains an unappeasable surplus. Freud, for his part, would no doubt find in Bloch's ideal future an image of the irrevocably lost past of the infant. In fact, it is not hard to see Bloch's *Totum* as something of a fetish, one that stands in for an unbearable absence. There is a sense in which hope for him is precious because it spells the death of desire. 'The urging', he remarks, 'does not continue endlessly unsatisfied.'[35]

Hope preserves something of the purblindness of desire, the fact that it never really knows what it is seeking; but it also gives it an affirmative twist, and by doing so plugs its unnerving lack. Its object is nothing less than the *Totum*, which lends it a grandiose enough goal; but since this aim is so all-inclusive as to be nothing very specific, hope retains something of desire's indeterminacy, and along with it its imposingly absolute quality. It is not to be reduced to the merely empirical, which is no doubt one reason why the Blochian future is so troublingly ill-defined. To specify it more closely would be for hope, the heroic protagonist of Bloch's work, to descend to the level of mere sublunary aspirations. If it is to avoid being confused with our more mundane desires, it must be incapable of stating exactly what it wants.

If reality is change and growth, why should an absolute future ever arrive? Bloch regards matter as perpetually unfinished, but one should not take this to imply that it could ever be completed. Unfinishedness is of its nature. It is not that matter has yet to perfect itself, but that it would not be matter if it did. How then can the *telos* of history be at odds with the process that gives it birth? Bloch writes of 'the *Totum* of a hope that puts the whole world into rapport with a total perfection',[36] but he overlooks the relation between human discontent and the material nature of reality. Only by the abolition of matter itself could tragedy be transcended. The death of desire would spell the death of humanity. There may indeed be plenty of perfection. But not for us.

4

Hope Against Hope

Jonathan Lear's *Radical Hope* records how Plenty Coups, the last great chief of the American Crow tribe, saw that his people's way of life was on the brink of a catastrophic collapse, and that 'in order to survive – and perhaps to flourish again – the Crow had to be willing to give up almost everything they understood about the good life' with no assurance of a successful outcome.[1] Ravaged by disease, devastated by the rival Sioux and Blackfeet, and almost bereft of their buffalo, the Crow lost nearly two-thirds of their number in the 1890s before they were finally herded onto a reservation. Plenty Coups had received in a dream a divine appeal to accept the ruin of his tribe's way of life, in the trust that only in this way could his people struggle through to a good end. His hope, in Lear's words, was that 'even with the death of the traditional forms of Crow subjectivity, the Crow can nevertheless survive and flourish again'.[2] One thinks of Job's words to Yahweh: 'Even if you kill me, I will have hope in you.'

Through a radical dissolution, one which the chief had not the slightest wish to see take place, the good life might be won back, even if Plenty Coups himself had no more than a glimmering of what that might mean. In his view, to hope was to recognise that there were possibilities that surpassed what could currently be conceived. Faith and hope are most needed where knowledge is hard to come by. 'When the buffalo went away', Plenty Coups remarked, 'the hearts of my people fell to the ground and they could not lift them up again. After that, nothing happened.'³ The departure of the buffalo heralded the end of history. As Lear argues, the Crow had lost the concepts with which they might construct a narrative. Since the schema that determined what counted as an event had been shattered, there was nothing more to recount. Yet the death of 'Crow subjectivity', as Lear calls it, might clear the ground for rebirth, so that history might begin to happen once more.

The decisions that the chief confronted were not ones that could be reasoned about in existing moral terms. Only afterwards, when a new matrix of understanding had emerged from the cataclysm, might the significance of his hope become clear to him. A storm is approaching, Plenty Coups dreams, but the devastation that it will wreak will only be understood retrospectively, in the light of concepts that will themselves have been transformed by the impending turmoil. Radical hope, Lear writes, 'anticipates a good for which those who have the hope as yet lack the appropriate concepts with which to understand it'. 'A culture', he comments, 'does not tend to train its young to endure its own breakdown',⁴ so that an inability to conceive of its own destruction will generally be one of its blind spots. In what conceivable metalanguage could a civilisation take the full measure of its own nonexistence, a situation which it could properly grasp only by leaping outside its own skin?⁵ Given the collapse of the tribe's interpretative framework, any very determinate form of hope was no longer possible. As T. S. Eliot might have put it, hope in this situation would undoubtedly have been hope for the wrong thing. Like Abraham with his knife to Isaac's throat, then, Plenty Coups was committed to a view of the good that transcended his own ability to grasp it. He was thrown back on what we have previously called fundamental or unconditional hope.

Revolutionary upheavals transform the very hermeneutical frames within which they occur, so that the attempt to understand them adequately must always be deferred. It is an exemplary case of Hegel's late-flying Owl of Minerva. 'If a people genuinely are at the historical limit of their way of life', Lear observes, 'there is precious little they can do to "peek over to the other side". Precisely because they are about to endure a historical rupture, the detailed texture of life on the other side has to be beyond their ken.'[6] It is in this spirit that Marx begins his *Eighteenth Brumaire of Louis Bonaparte* by aiming a satirical shaft at those revolutionaries who draw their symbolic resources from the past, rather than being attuned to what he cryptically calls 'the poetry of the future'. If radical transformation is a hard concept to seize, it is because it demands foresight and lucidity, precision and calculation, but all in the name of an end that is necessarily opaque. To project a future is inevitably to draw upon the experience of the present, and thus to fail to surpass what we know already; yet how otherwise can a future which exceeds our present understanding be brought to birth? How could we even identify a future that was entirely discontinuous with the past, any more than we could know that utterly alien beings were swarming through our living rooms?

Despite this, Plenty Coups regarded himself as having reason to hope for a dignified passage across the abyss dividing present and future. He was, as it happens, a baptised Christian, one who regarded his commitment to God as sustaining his trust in a future that outstripped his own efforts to grasp it. Even so, he was enough of a realist to recognise that there was no necessity for the Crow way of life to carry on, and that death would be preferable to certain conceivable outcomes. In the event, his faith served him well: the tribe finally accepted life on a reservation, but some of their land was eventually returned to them by the US government. As Einstein remarked, if a thing does not seem absurd at first, there is no hope for it.

As the case of Plenty Coups illustrates, the most authentic kind of hope is whatever can be salvaged, stripped of guarantees, from a general dissolution. It represents an irreducible residue that refuses to give way, plucking its resilience from an openness to the possibility of unmitigated disaster. It is thus as remote from optimism as could be imagined. It also stands at a wary remove from the buoyant universe of Ernst Bloch. It is not, to be sure, that every empirical hope need be of this kind. One's hope for fine weather tomorrow is not compelled to pass through some dark night of the soul in which the possibility of a tsunami is glumly contemplated. It is rather that this mode of hope, not least when it comes to political history, is a paradigm of hope in general – which is to say, paradoxically, that the exemplary case of hope is tragedy. Or, at least, the kind of tragedy in which hope is a question of whatever manages to survive the general catastrophe. There are, to be sure, tragic actions in both art and reality in which there is nothing in the end to yield solace to the disconsolate. Nothing flourished as a result of the Nazi camps. Even so, there can be no tragedy without a sense of value, whether or not that value actually bears fruit. We would not call tragic the destruction of something we did not prize. If tragedy cuts deeper than pessimism, it is because its horror is laced with an enriched sense of human worth. Perhaps we could pass beyond tragedy entirely only by abandoning the view that there is anything to be cherished in the first place, in which case we might prefer to tarry with it.

Hope, then, is what survives the general ruin – though this, in the case of Shakespeare's *King Lear*, would seem to be little or nothing. Yet the word 'nothing' has an affirmative resonance in the play as well as an ominous one. When Cordelia utters it to her father as the drama opens, it is a mark of authenticity, in contrast to the mendacious rhetoric of her sisters Goneril and Regan:

Lear: . . . what can you say to draw
A third more opulent than your sisters? Speak.
Cordelia: Nothing, my lord.
Lear: Nothing?
Cordelia: Nothing.
Lear: Nothing will come of nothing: speak again.

Cordelia: Unhappy that I am, I cannot heave
My heart into my mouth: I love your majesty
According to my bond, no more nor less.

(act 1, scene 1)

Cordelia's 'Nothing' is factually exact: when language has been stretched beyond all measure by her duplicitous sisters, there is indeed no way in which she can verbally outflank them. When a genuine nullity (Goneril and Regan's lack of love for their father) has been inflated to everything, only a deflationary nothing can restore some sense of the real. As the drama runs its course, we shall see how this is also true of the therapeutic fictions that Edgar, Kent and the Fool fashion for the mad Lear and the deceived Gloucester – charades, illusions and improvised bits of theatre which wrench language out of joint in the manner of Lear's lying daughters, but now in the name of restoring the king and his distraught courtier to their senses. Goneril and Regan set the truth at nothing, while for Cordelia nothing is the truth. The word, tolling like a doleful bell through the opening lines of the play, sounds the note of moral realism that Lear needs if he is not to founder.

Cordelia is also meticulous in addressing Lear's actual question. He does not ask what she can say to assure him of her love, but (by implication) what outrageous hyperbole she can produce in excess of her sisters' bloated speech. For her part, Cordelia does not mean that she can say nothing to convey her love, but that she is struck dumb in the discursive context her father has manufactured for her. It is the deluded Lear who chooses to hear her scrupulously accurate response as a declaration of indifference. As greedy for unbounded affection from his children as an infant is from its parents, he has fashioned a piece of theatre within which his daughter's speech is bound to be nullified. In asking her to speak, then, he simultaneously silences her. Ask a loaded question and you receive a dusty answer. Lear's moral arithmetic, however ('Nothing will come of nothing'), will prove to be spurious as the drama unfolds. On the contrary, something, if it is finally to emerge, can do so only from the ruins of some illusory all. Only by accepting his own fleshliness and infirmity has Lear any hope of groping his way beyond them.

The punctiliousness of Cordelia's 'Nothing' chimes with the exactitude of the word 'bond'. Unusually, the word 'nothing' here signifies a kind of determinacy, a question of constraints and distinctions, while in a parallel way 'bond' suggests a definitive form of love. Here as in *The Merchant of Venice*, Shakespeare is playing on the double sense of 'bond', as both formal contract and fleshly union. Lear can see only an evasive reticence in his daughter's precision, blind to the fact that an affection inspired by traditional obligation is likely to prove more fruitful and enduring than one at the mercy of erotic impulse or subjective whim. For Cordelia to love Lear according to her bond is to love him as a devoted daughter.

Cordelia's 'Nothing' is a salvo against surplus, as the play meditates on the contrast between forms of superfluity which are life-giving (grace, forgiveness, a rejection of mean-spirited utility, a belief that surpassing the measure is normative for human beings) and those which are ruinous. At one point, Kent describes his own mode of speech as 'the modest truth, / Nor more nor clipped, but so' (act 4, scene 6), an equipoise denied to the Cordelia of the opening scene, who is forced into clippedness by the surfeit of her siblings. It is, however, an equipoise hard to achieve in general, since it is a mark of humanity to be superfluous or self-surpassing by its very nature, producing an excess over determinate need to which we give the name of history, culture or desire:

> *Lear:* O reason not the need! Our basest beggars
> Are in the poorest things superfluous.
> Allow not nature more than nature needs,
> Man's life is cheap as beasts.
>
> (act 2, scene 2)

The more destructive modes of prodigality in *Lear* include 'surplus' in the economic sense of the term, which like a second layer of flesh swaddles the rich from feeling the wretchedness of

the poor, and thus prevents them from taking action to allevi-
ate it. In Lear's view, this form of surplus is ripe for economic
redistribution:

> Poor naked wretches, wheresoe'er you are,
> How shall your houseless heads and unfed sides,
> Your looped and windowed raggedness, defend you
> From seasons such as these? O, I have ta'en
> Too little care of this! Take physic, pomp,
> Expose thyself to feel what wretches feel,
> That thou mayst shake the superflux to them,
> And show the heavens more just.
>
> (act 3, scene 4)

Lear's newfound solidarity with the destitute involves what one
might call the politics of nothingness. In being forced to confront his own fragility, he is able to invest himself once more
with representative status, no longer as king but as a type of the
dispossessed.

If Lear himself is forced through this painful self-divestiture
by circumstance, Edgar freely appropriates it:

> I will preserve myself, and am bethought
> To take the basest and most poorest shape
> That ever penury in contempt of man
> Brought near to beast: my face I'll grime with filth,
> Blanket my loins, elf all my hairs in knots,
> And with presented nakedness outface
> The winds and persecutions of the sky . . .
>   . . . Poor Turlygod, poor Tom!
> That's something yet: Edgar I nothing am.
>
> (act 2, scene 2)

Edgar, who is an outcast in any case, is the kind of tragic protagonist who makes his destiny his choice, embracing and even
parodying his own dispossession, yet (since he does so by virtue
of a free decision) transcending it in that very act. Like Cordelia
in the eyes of her husband, France, he is 'most rich, being poor'.
It is thus that he is able to survive at the end of the play, one

of a paltry number of leading characters to do so. His brother Edmund also flourishes, for a while at least, by stooping to constraint, but in his case to the rigours of his own predatory nature. Like many a Shakespearean villain, he is a full-blooded cynic and naturalist for whom moral value is a mere conventional construct with no grounding in the real, and Nature (including his own appetites) neutral, rigorously deterministic stuff – stuff which can nonetheless be manipulated to one's advantage once one has apprised oneself of its unalterable laws. It is to this conception of Nature, one on which nurture or culture will never stick, that Edmund holds one should be loyal – an incoherent belief, to be sure, since there is nothing in Nature thus defined that might motivate such fidelity to it. It is not clear, in other words, whether conformity to Nature is a fact or a value. If Edmund's villainy is the upshot of a moral decision, one might admire its audacity while suspecting that it undercuts his deterministic views; if he cannot help being the moral ruffian he is, his philosophy holds up while our admiration for his impudence collapses.

In his own opinion, Edmund is incapable of being anything but himself. As such, he has an ironic affinity with Cordelia, though unlike her he can dissemble his nature in order to gratify its demands. Being able to disguise what he is is part of what he is, an aspect of his immutable identity. Like animal camouflage, it is one of the ways a savagely amoral Nature allows him to prevail. Much the same is true of Iago. This is not the case with Goneril and Regan, who after their initial subterfuge prove incapable of transgressing their own fixed natures in all the most destructive of ways. Though they can practise a false kind of superfluity in their grandiloquent flattery of their father, they take no delight in the purely gratuitous. Like Lear, their moral arithmetic is flawed, unable as they are to grasp why their father should want a retinue of a hundred knights when he has no strict need of them. Unlike Cordelia's, their precision is cruel, automated and inhuman.

Is there any hope in the play? Cordelia, after all, dies, despite the fact that she survives in all of Shakespeare's original sources for the story, and most of the other major figures either perish or emerge chastened and diminished. But one should not attend simply to what the play itself calls the 'horror' of a conclusion, as though hope were a purely teleological affair. There may even be a sense in which the deaths of Lear and Cordelia sardonically undercut this expectation, admonishing us not to pitch all on our sense of an ending. There is hope, for example, in the fact that the cheerless finale we witness is by no means predestined. To this extent, the drama itself seems not to share Edmund's truculent determinism. It is not hard to see how things might have worked out differently, had Lear not been so stiff-necked. 'A radical contingency haunts every story of tragedy', writes Stanley Cavell, a claim which is not universally true (there are tragedies of fate), but which is true enough of *Lear*.[7] There may be scant hope at the end of Lear's narrative, but neither was there any good reason for it to get started in the first place. In this sense, battered and bloodied survivors like Edgar and Kent might well claim that there is plenty of hope, but not for them.

Contingency and indeterminacy may help to breed tragedy, as they do in the fiction of Thomas Hardy, but they can also point up its avoidability. What the philosopher Quentin Meillassoux sees as the manifest gratuitousness of the given can undo false versions of necessity, and with them a spurious sense of tragic fatality. In Meillassoux's view, it is atheism which lies at the root of hope, since the death of God signals the death of necessity and the birth of contingency, and as long as there is contingency there is hope.[8] 'The words "the divine inexistence"', he remarks, 'clear and pure as moonlight, guarantee hope so long as a just person remains in existence.'[9] There is hope as long as history lacks closure. If the past was different from the present, so may the future be.

Lear dies, though hardly in despair. His conviction that Cordelia still breathes may be an illusion, but it might also be seen as a promise of resurrection. Commenting on the scene, Walter Stein reminds us that 'the classic emblem of Christian redemption is itself an unstirring, executed body'.[10] Those like Lear who become unhinged from reality by hubris and self-serving fantasy need to be broken and refashioned, beaten down to whatever fleshly residue of themselves they are finally unable to disown; and the fact there is no guarantee that one will survive this process intact does not negate its value. To shed one's self-deceptions may not be to flourish, but in tragic art it is generally a precondition of it. Even if his final words express a false hope, Lear fares better in this respect than those tragic figures, from Shakespeare's Othello to Ibsen's Master Builder and Arthur Miller's Willy Loman, who march to their deaths still more or less self-deceived, and whose condition is in this sense more critical than that of the remorseful and clear-eyed. Able at last to confront his own false consciousness, Lear repents and petitions humbly for forgiveness, which is more than can be said of Macbeth or Miss Julie. The fact that neither he nor Cordelia manages to survive fails to sabotage this value. Nor can the deaths of the leading characters undermine the integrity of the poetry that records them. In this sense, the play's own artistry stands in judgment on any too facile disenchantment.

We have seen already that the work itself contains various surreal fictions and charades; and these, as with Gloucester's illusory plunge off the symbolic extremity of Dover cliff, are for the most part cases of art in the service of reality. A deranged monarch, a sorely distracted courtier, a professional Fool, a young nobleman pretending to be out of his mind, and an aristocrat disguised as a plain-speaking commoner weave a mesh of grotesque fantasies that furnish a Lear and Gloucester with their sole remaining access to the truth. It is as though the king is so sunk in delusion that his condition cannot be tackled head-on, only dismantled from within in a conspiracy of fools and madmen. When truth itself becomes fraudulent, only a homeopathic admixture of illusion can restore it.

In fashioning these heuristic fictions, the play makes an oblique allusion to its own therapeutic powers. In articulating the extremity to which its protagonist is brought, tragedy is by that very act able to gaze beyond it. One thinks of Bertolt Brecht's remark in *The Messingkauf Dialogues*: 'Language by means of sounds, or better still words, is a vast liberation, because it means the sufferer is beginning to produce something. He's already mixing his sorrow with an account of the blows he has received; he's already making something out of the utterly devastating. Observation has set in.'[11] In tragedy, writes Roland Barthes in *Sur Racine*, one never dies because one is always talking. To name a disaster is to mark its limits and lend it a palpable shape, so that, as Yeats writes of *Hamlet* and *Lear* in 'Lapis Lazuli', 'It cannot grow by an inch or an ounce.' There can be no more adversity for Lear or Hamlet beyond what we witness on stage. In this sense, the play itself marks an absolute end to its protagonist's sorrows, as art itself becomes an image of the death with which it deals. One might claim, even so, that in seeking to redeem suffering in symbolic form, tragedy is in danger of enfeebling its force. Wedded to shapeliness, it finds it hard to cope with the random and amorphous.

When tragic art is pressed to an extreme, life either ceases altogether or begins to stir once more. When Edgar exclaims that 'the worst is not / So long as we can say "This is the worst"', it might appear that it is the latter possibility he has in mind. As long as calamity can be given a voice, it ceases to be the final word. Hope would stumble to a halt only when we could no longer identify cruelty and injustice for what they were. To speak of hopelessness must logically presuppose the idea of hope. It is when meaning as such collapses that tragedy is no longer possible; so that if *King Lear* itself continues to thrive as an artistic event, it is testimony to the fact that the catastrophe cannot yet have come about. There would seem to be no 'worst' in the writing of Samuel Beckett, since one can always disintegrate a bit more, feel yet another limb stiffening up, slip another inch or so into decrepitude, rather as Gerard Manley Hopkins finds himself pitched vertiginously in one of his darker sonnets from one pang of despair to another, with no end in sight. Yet neither in the case of Beckett is there any death or definitive closure, as language continues to grope its way forward like a blind beggar. 'If despair prompts speech or reasoning', Albert Camus comments, 'and above all if it results in writing, fraternity is established, natural objects are justified, love is born. A literature of despair is a contradiction in terms.'[12]

For us to be able to speak of a cataclysm means that there must be something that survives it, even if it is no more than a distraught messenger or a scrap of paper. For Plenty Coups to report that things stopped happening when the buffalo left is in one sense self-refuting, since this very declaration counts as an event, however mournful and meagre. Speech, and the capacity to bear witness, staggers on. The end of everything could leave no legacy, despite those American Evangelicals who were planning some years ago to film the Second Coming and pondering which camera angles (Antarctica? the Equator?) might prove the most productive. In a similar way, death is not an event for those who undergo it, but the end of narrativity as such.

As Edgar observes a few lines earlier,

> . . . To be worst,
> The lowest and most dejected thing of fortune,
> Stands still in esperance, lives not in fear;
> The lamentable change is from the best,
> The worst returns to laughter.
>
> (act 4, scene 1)

The worst is in some perverse sense a source of hope, bringing as it does the assurance that one can sink no further. One may now relax, since no amount of effort is likely to repair one's condition. One calls to mind the conundrum in which one speaker insists to another, 'Things can't get any worse', to which the other replies, 'Oh yes, they can.' Which of them is the optimist and which the pessimist? 'If one has settled into the worst position, the lowest and most forgotten by fortune', writes Enrique Vila-Matas in his novel *Dublinesque*, 'one can always still hope and not live in fear.' Max Horkheimer comments in his *Critique of Instrumental Reason* that Schopenhauer knows more than any other thinker of hope precisely because he confronts a condition of utter hopelessness.[13] For Pascal, the very direness of our condition is an ironic source of hope, since it suggests just what resources of divine grace must lie to hand to remedy it. Malcolm Bull speaks of the Muselmen or living dead of the Nazi concentration camps as 'redeemed by their own hopelessness', invulnerable to hope and therefore to hurt.[14] Power can have no hold over those who are oblivious to its stratagems. Men and women who have nothing to lose, like the beggar whose persona Edgar adopts, or like the psychopathic Barnadine in *Measure for Measure*, may prove to be fearless, invulnerable and therefore dangerous. Pressed to an extreme, self-dispossession can capsize into a curious kind of freedom, as something rich and rare is born of nothing.

As long as there is language, then, hope remains possible; yet this is not in fact what Edgar has in mind. He is warning of what misfortunes may still be to come, foreseeing a condition in which even the ability to give tongue to the horror would be denied us. As Sophocles' Philoctetes is aware, what is especially resistant to speech is pain. Genuine tragedy would pass beyond tragedy, striking it as dumb as Lear strikes Cordelia. The true calamity would involve the extinction of the word. Hope is extinguished when language is obliterated. It is not true that language can repair one's condition simply by lending a name to it, but it is true that one cannot repair it without doing so. Marx's celebrated eleventh thesis on Feuerbach, which insists on the need to change the world rather than interpret it, seems on the face of it not to recognise that the latter is an essential precondition of the former.

'Only one thing remained reachable, close and secure amid all losses: language', writes Paul Celan of the concentration camps. 'Yes, language. In spite of everything, it remained secure against loss.'[15] But this, too, can fail altogether. Its insulation against loss is by no means iron-clad. There are those who see the horrors of the Holocaust as beggaring all speech, and as such beyond the scope of tragic art. Whereas the careers of Hamlet or Hedda Gabler are well delineated, since these figures exist only as determinate textual patterns, an event like the Holocaust resists any such design. Even so, one might seek to combine the two contending senses of Edgar's speech. Could we not name a condition in which we would be beyond all sense, yet in the act of naming it attempt to come to terms with it? This is not out of the question. Those who are diagnosed with dementia, and are aware that in some years' time they will be beyond all coherent speech, may still muster the resources to carry on.

Despite Edgar's misgivings, there would seem hope enough in Shakespeare's last comedies, as lost children are found, past enmities reconciled, the wicked brought to repentance, dead wives miraculously resurrected, Nature portrayed as a regenerative force, and old injuries erased by the healing action of time. The death of Cordelia yields ground to the return to life of Hermione in *The Winter's Tale*. Yet there would seem no redemption in these later dramas without the aid of grace, art, magic and miracle. Left to their own devices, history and politics appear unlikely to usher in the New Jerusalem. You need to stray beyond these domains – to the countryside, a remote island, the common people, myth and fairy tale, the restorative cycles of Nature, the younger generation, the regenerative power of the ocean – for the resources that might renew them. The gorgeously inventive verse of *The Winter's Tale* holds an ugly reality at arm's length, stylising and compacting the tragic action. Prospero in *The Tempest* may rout his enemies and regain his kingdom, but only because he wields preternatural powers denied to Timon or Büchner's Danton. We are supposed to take these powers as symbolic of art itself, yet art can reconcile and transfigure only within the confines of a text or a theatre. In this sense, there is a certain pessimism about Prospero's enchanted staff, just as there is about the nonrealist setting of the play itself. On a magic island, as in a work of fiction, one can grant a certain free play to the forces of evil in order to master them on one's own terms, a far less plausible project in reality. There is conflict and danger, to be sure, but these things are cast from the outset in the form of their prospective resolution. Even then, however, the tragedy of the past cannot be repaired altogether, any more than the death of the child Mamillius can be undone at the end of *The Winter's*

Tale. In fact, no death can be annulled. Even the risen body of Jesus bears the marks of his execution.

Perhaps, though, the cunning devices of the last comedies are realist after all. They symbolise not only art but grace, which for Shakespeare and his audiences was doubtless real enough. If magical spirits and moving statues are more than theatrical artifice, it is because they are intended as allegories of a deeper mode of transcendence. Shakespeare's drama would seem to credit the Catholic doctrine that grace perfects nature rather than abolishing it. There is no salvation in human nature itself, but that nature is hospitable to its own self-transcendence. The dynamic by which humanity can reach beyond itself is one that is built into its condition. This is why Nietzsche is mistaken to admonish his readers to 'remain faithful to the earth, and [not to] believe those who speak to you of otherworldly hopes'.[16] On the contrary, it is an attachment to the present that motivates one's hope for a changed future, so that to be faithful to what we have is to trust to its transfiguration.

There is a degree of pessimism in the fact that Nature cannot transcend itself by virtue of its own powers, but a modicum of hope in the fact that the grace which transforms it is a potential within it, rather as art has a foundation in the material reality it reconfigures. Art can reshape that reality, as grace can transfigure nature, but it is also a product of what it works upon. It is a dialectic captured in Polixenes' words in *The Winter's Tale:*

> Yet nature is made better by no mean
> But nature makes that mean, so over that art,
> Which you say adds to nature, is an art
> That nature makes . . .
>   . . . this is an art
> Which does mend nature, change it rather, though
> The art itself is nature.
>
>   (act 4, scene 4)

The work of art is one mode in which Nature furnishes the means of its own transformation. Yet this is not true of the relations between Nature and grace, so that there is a slippage here between image and reality. Grace may be implicit in human nature, but it is not a product of it. Instead, it is a divine gift bestowed from beyond the frontiers of secular history. And this disjuncture between the two domains is bound to qualify any too ingenuous hope. One should not despair, because grace is not foreign to humanity; one should not presume, because it is not an organic process as spontaneous as the blooming of a rose. The last comedies hold a vision of 'great creating nature' in tension with Edmund's darker view of the natural, which is why hope must be suitably tempered. Otherwise one underestimates the depravity of what needs to be redeemed, buying one's transcendence on the cheap. There are always unregenerate souls like Malvolio who refuse to be drawn into the comic denouement, and in doing so remind us of its limits. Comic resolutions can also be staged in a way that draws ironic attention to their artifice. The virtuous are rewarded and the vicious packed off empty-handed, but only because we are in a theatre.

Yet there is Perdita's sense of nature as well, which is a potentially more subversive affair than that of either Edmund or Polixenes. When the latter pulls rank in order to break up the play's young lovers, Perdita declares that

I was not much afeard, for once or twice
I was about to speak and tell him plainly,
The selfsame sun that shines upon his court
Hides not his visage from our cottage but
Looks on alike.

(act 4, scene 4)

Nature, as Edmund maintains, may know nothing of moral distinctions, but neither does it respect social ones. There is a rough-and-ready egalitarianism about it which poses a threat to the prevailing power structure. Part of the play's strategy, then, is to neutralise the dangers involved in importing regenerative resources from the common life into the court by ensuring that Perdita, who speaks up for the natural equality of men and women, has unknown to herself been a courtly insider all along. She is a princess as well as a peasant. For a member of the common people to prove worthy of being raised to noble status, since she is secretly an aristocrat in any case, is an appropriate image of how grace is potentially at work within the Nature it exalts.

∝⁂∝

Buying one's transcendence on the cheap is not a fault one can lay at Kierkegaard's door. In *The Sickness Unto Death*, despair is to be affirmed as well as lamented, since it is by this means that salvation can be dearly bought, in contrast with some off-the-peg optimism. The opposite of hope may be a callow cheerfulness, but it is certainly not tragedy. 'Despair', Kierkegaard writes, 'is that sickness of which it is true that it is the greatest misfortune never to have had it; it is truly providential to get it, even though it is the most dangerous of all sicknesses if one does not want to be cured of it.'[17] Curiously enough, there is infinite merit in being able to abandon hope. The self, Kierkegaard remarks, 'is only healthy and free from despair when, precisely by having despaired, it is grounded transparently in God'.[18] The capacity to despair represents humanity's edge over the beasts, and as such figures as a kind of *felix culpa* without which one would be altogether bereft of spirit. Those in despair long to be autonomous but cannot achieve this condition; and this itself is a negative index of hope, pointing as it does to the imperishable self which they are unable to make their own. To arrive at the truth, Kierkegaard writes, 'one has to pass through every negativity; it is just as the old story says about breaking a certain magic spell: it won't be broken until the piece is played right through backwards'.[19] To repent, one 'must first despair with a vengeance, despair to the full, so that the life of the spirit can break through from the ground up'.[20]

It is a familiar form of spiritual elitism, to be found all the way from Baudelaire to Graham Greene. On this view, most men and women, like Eliot's hollow men, are too spiritually vacuous even to be damned. If they had a closer acquaintance with Satan, they might know a little of God. Only those endowed with a distinctive selfhood are capable of recognising how that self is grounded in eternity, but such authentic individuality is hard to come by. 'The surest way to destroy a man', comments the Provost in Ibsen's *Brand*, 'is to turn him into an individual', a view that as far as run-of-the-mill humanity goes Kierkegaard would thoroughly endorse. Those who despair, unlike the bovine masses, at least bear witness to their own moral inwardness. As full-bloodedly metaphysical beings, they are on intimate terms with the saints, and as such superior to what one might call the moral middle classes. One might call it the *Brighton Rock* syndrome. Hopelessness is in this sense a badge of honour. Only those steadfast enough to appropriate their eternal selves can confront the prospect of their absolute loss, and in doing so display a spirit worthy of salvation. Viewed in this light, despair comes to seem almost as precious as paradise. There is little sense that Kierkegaard takes the measure of its sheer horror, in the manner of Thomas Mann's *Doctor Faustus*. Instead, it is an essential prelude to divine grace, a *sine qua non* of spiritual growth.

All the same, Kierkegaard grasps something of the tragic paradox of both faith and hope. With Abraham's sacrifice of Isaac in mind, he speaks of those who believe as being convinced of their own undoing, yet trusting to the fact that this is somehow not the last word. 'The contradiction here', he writes, 'is that in human terms the undoing is certain and that still there is possibility.'[21] That this is more than simply illogical is borne out by Viktor Frankl's counsel that the victims of concentration camps should not lose hope, 'but should keep their courage in the certainty that the hopelessness of our struggle does not detract from its dignity and value'.[22] Hope, once more, is not simply a teleological affair. It is possible to lose hope but not to despair. As with tragedy, value is a question not simply of one's fate but of the relationship one establishes with it. At the very least, one can always hope that others might learn from one's plight. Like culture or education, one can bequeath hope as a legacy to posterity while being stripped of it oneself. When St Augustine writes that 'hope has for its object only what is good, only what is future, and only what affects the man who entertains the hope',[23] he is mistaken on all three counts. There are those, for example, who make a gift of their deaths to those who come after them, so that something fruitful may come of failure.

In *Living in the End Times*, Slavoj Žižek quotes an exchange between Spartacus and a pirate in Stanley Kubrick's film *Spartacus* in which the pirate asks the slave leader whether he is aware that his rebellion is doomed. Will he and his men continue to fight to the end, even in the face of inevitable defeat? Spartacus replies that the slaves' struggle is not simply to improve their condition, but a principled rebellion in the name of freedom; so that even if they are all slaughtered, their insurrection will not have been in vain. On the contrary, it will have manifested their unconditional commitment to emancipation. As Žižek remarks, 'Their act of rebellion itself, whatever the outcome, already counts as a success.'[24] The price Spartacus and his comrades would pay for surviving without a struggle would be their integrity. There are occasions when men and women must die in order to defend a principle that makes life worth living. There is more at stake in acting than dismal or agreeable outcomes. One would not refuse a glass of water to a man trapped under a roof beam simply because one knew that the rest of the building was about to fall in on him and finish him off. Hope can acknowledge loss or destruction to be unavoidable, which is where it differs from some currents of optimism, yet still refuse to capitulate. One can retain a degree of dignity and integrity, refraining, in Gabriel Marcel's words, from going to pieces. One would not wish to add spice to one's enemy's victory by yielding him the pleasure of seeing you in a blind panic. In this sense of non-despair, one might regard humanity as doomed while still having faith in the human spirit. 'Even though all is lost, we are not' might serve as the motto of this refusal to give way. As Friedrich Schelling writes of tragic hope, 'One thing still remains – to know that it is an objective power that threatens to destroy our freedom and, with this firm

and certain conviction in our hearts, to fight against it, to sum-
mon up all our freedom and thus to perish.'[25]

For Walter Benjamin, suspending the fruits of action means
blasting an event out of the continuum of history, and in doing
so anticipating one's death. It is at the point of death above all
that consequences cease to be important, at least for oneself, and
that actions can thus be executed for their own sake. One should
try to see how one's acts might appear from the standpoint of
eternity, treating every one as though it were one's last, folding
the future into the present rather than (as with historicism) folding the past into the present and future. In this way one can live
ironically, standing in and out of history at the same time, in
the manner of those in St Paul's First Epistle to the Corinthians
'who deal with the world as though they had no dealings with the
world'. It is a stance as typical of the revolutionary as it is of the
monk. As Theodor Adorno writes, 'The only philosophy which
can be responsibly practiced is the attempt to contemplate all
things as they would present themselves from the standpoint of
redemption.'[26] In any case, all actions have the finality of death
about them, since for good or ill they cannot be undone.

All this has a bearing on the political left. One of the issues
it raises too rarely is: what if it were to fail? The left's nervous-
ness of the query is understandable, given that it would seem
at a stroke to demoralise its members and lend comfort to its
opponents. There are many leftists for whom pessimism is consequently as much a thought crime as it is for those motivational
speakers who are paid to convince US corporate executives that
they are demigods in disguise. 'A Marxist does not have the right
to be pessimistic', writes Ernst Bloch,[27] as if a sober estimate that
one can make no gains in this or that situation were some kind
of spiritual betrayal. With a bright-eyed self-deception that even
Matt Ridley might envy, there are always revolutionary opportu-
nities to hand for some enthusiastic radicals, if only one had the
boldness to seize them. This therapeutic fiction has seen a good
many militants through the darkest nights of the class struggle.

The alarming instability of capitalism, which is indeed a source of encouragement to its antagonists, is appropriately underlined, but not the fact that the system has rather more tanks at its disposal than its opponents.

The struggle for a just society involves an instrumental rationality, but it is not only that. The left would continue to protest against sweated labour and mass unemployment even if it were morally certain that capitalism is here to stay. Bertolt Brecht speaks in his poem 'An die Nachgeborenen' of despairing only where there is injustice and no rebellion; but even if rebellion were to evaporate altogether, the fact that men and women have fought for their freedom so tenaciously over the centuries would still be a source of value. There would still, so to speak, be something to be salvaged on Judgment Day. Though justice may not flourish in the end, a life devoted to the pursuit of it remains a creditable one. Not to succeed in the end is not necessarily to have failed, any more than it is true that all's well that ends well. It is only the lure of teleology that persuades us of this fallacy. Even if history were to fall into utter ruin, it would be a matter for despair only if that catastrophe were predestined; and even then it is possible, like many a tragic protagonist, to pluck value from combating the inevitable. Indeed, unless one combats the inevitable, one will never know how inevitable it was in the first place. The truth, however, is that catastrophe is not written into the march of history, any more than hope is. However desolate the future may prove, it might always have been different. The contingency that can make for misfortune can also make for success. As Aristotle appreciates, the reason why things can decline (mutability) is also the reason why they can prosper. Besides, a lamentable future would almost certainly be the handiwork of a rapacious ruling minority, not the product of humanity as a whole.

Despite all this, one does not need to view hope in excessively existential terms. Goals are indeed important. Benjamin's philosophy of history, for all its spiritual wisdom, represents an overreaction to the idea of historical progress, one understandable in its context. Messianism of Benjamin's kind has too little faith in history. As Fredric Jameson comments, 'You would not evoke the messianic in a genuinely revolutionary period, a period in which changes can be sensed at work all around you; the messianic does not mean immediate hope in that sense, perhaps not even hope against hope; it is a unique variety of the species "hope" that scarcely bears any of the latter's normal characteristics and that flourishes only in a time of absolute hopelessness.'[28] Nor does one need to view hope in too absolute or unconditional terms. Bloch is mistaken to imagine that it is a question of all or nothing. According to psychoanalytic theory, we shall never be cured of desire, but this is not to say that we cannot strike a diplomatic pact with it. Though there will be no utopia, in the sense of a world purged of discord and dissatisfaction, it is sober realism to believe that our condition could be mightily improved. It is not that all will be well, but that all might be well enough. One does not need a breed of archangels in order to refrain from genocide or put paid to the trafficking of sex slaves. It is those who deny this good sense who are the fantasists, whatever their vaunted pragmatism. Nothing is more otherworldly than the assumption that the world as we know it is here to stay.

Yet though hope need not in general cut to the foundations, it is just this variety of it that is needed for radical change, given the formidable resistance such a project would confront. In the end, one would need what the theologian Herbert McCabe calls a hope that 'goes through defeat and crucifixion to resurrection'.[29] Or as Raymond Williams puts it in rather more secular terms: 'The fact is that neither the frankly utopian form, nor even the more qualified outlines of practicable futures, can begin to flow until we have faced, at the necessary depth, the divisions and contradictions which now inhibit them.'[30] The singer Sinead O'Connor once remarked in the course of a television interview that she found the resurrection so much more joyful than the crucifixion, as though, like choosing a colour of scarf, one could plump for the one or the other option depending on one's temperament. It is the quintessence of optimism. She did not see that the resurrection is hopeful precisely because what it redeems is the agony and desolation of the cross.

⸙

It has been claimed that the bloodiest event in the history of humankind was the An Lushan revolt and civil war of eighth-century China, which on some estimates resulted in a staggering 429 million deaths.[31] The catastrophe is thought to have been responsible for the loss of two-thirds of the citizens of the Chinese empire, or a sixth of the world's population at the time. The Mongol conquests of the thirteenth century, with perhaps 278 million dead, come not far behind. Tamerlane may well have slaughtered five times as many men and women as Stalin, while the Thirty Years' War piled up around twice as many corpses as the First World War. The Second World War witnessed some 55 million deaths, and even the English Civil War may have wiped out almost half a million people. The extermination of the American Indians outdid Mao Zedong's massacres by a ratio of more than two to one. There were about 40 million deaths in battle during the twentieth century.

Many of our ancestors were very nasty indeed, as indeed are a number of our contemporaries. The Bible depicts a world of rape, plunder, torture, slavery and indiscriminate slaughter. The ancient Romans tied naked women to stakes to be raped or devoured by animals; St George was seated astride a sharp blade with weights tied to his legs, roasted over a fire, pierced through the feet, crushed on a spiked wheel, had sixty nails hammered into his head and was then sawn in half. To crown his indignities, he was later appointed patron of the Boy Scout movement. One atrocitologist reckons the death toll of the Crusades, proportionate to the global population of the time, to be about the same as the Holocaust. At various times in the past you could be put to death for gossiping, stealing cabbages, picking up sticks on the Sabbath, arguing with your parents or making critical remarks about the royal gardens. Until fairly recently, torture was not sporadic, clandestine or universally deplored, but systematic,

open to view, and even commended as an occasion for technological inventiveness.

It is not exactly a record to inspire hope. In fact, if this appalling din of hacking and gouging is to be attributed simply to
human nature, it is hard to see how there could be much prospect
of our condition improving. That it indeed involves human nature is not to be doubted. If human beings are capable of behav-
ing in this way, then it follows that they have it in their natures
to do so. This, then, is the bad news. The good news is that
that nature is by no means unconstrained. It is moulded by historical circumstance, which has not so far been greatly in our
favour. Politics throughout human history has been for the most
part violent and corrupt. Virtue, where it has flourished, has been
largely a private or minority affair. The poet Seamus Heaney
speaks in *The Cure at Troy* of those quasi-miraculous moments
when hope and history rhyme, but the relationship between the
two has more commonly resembled that of the line endings of
blank verse. This, however, is partly because men and women
have been forced to live under social systems that generate scarcity, violence and mutual antagonism. It is this which Marx has
in mind when he speaks of the whole of past history as weighing
like a nightmare on the brains of the living. And there is always
so much more of the past than there is of the present. It is always
liable, as in an Ibsen tragedy, to weigh in at a moment of crisis to
crush the prospect of an emancipated future.

In such conditions, men and women are unlikely to be at
their morally most impressive. Their less admirable inclinations
will tend to be exacerbated. This is not to suggest that if only
they were free of such pressures they would behave like cherubs.
There would no doubt still be a sizeable quota of thugs, sadists
and enthusiastic amateur torturers among the general citizenry.
The fact that a good deal of our disreputable behaviour is gen-
erated by the regimes under which we live does not let us off
the moral hook altogether. It was we, after all, who constructed
those regimes in the first place. Even so, it means that those who
are decent and good-hearted must practise these virtues against

the historical odds. In this sense, the moral experiment has been rigged. This is why, as with the doctrine of original sin, our bungling and belligerence are not to be laid entirely at our own door. That our woes are to a large extent systemic is in one sense cause for despondency, since systems can be formidably hard to change. But it is also grounds for hope. We do not know how much more morally resplendent we would be were these institutions to be changed. Perhaps not much. But we owe it to ourselves to find out. Those who speak of the darkness of men's hearts may not be so much wrong as premature. This, then, is the good news; the bad news is that there is no reason to assume that humanly created evils are in principle any more curable than natural ones. We will probably find a cure for cancer, but not for murder.

Tragic hope is hope in extremis. The concept of progress, Benjamin insists, must be grounded in the idea of catastrophe. The optimist cannot despair, but neither can he know genuine hope, since he disavows the conditions that make it essential. Erik Erikson, with the development of the small infant in mind, speaks of hope as 'the enduring belief in the attainability of fervent wishes, in spite of the dark urges and rages that mark the beginning of existence'.[32] Only through trust in the love of its carers can the child resist being claimed by those malign forces. At the end of Thomas Mann's *Doctor Faustus*, perhaps the most magnificent of all literary portraits of evil, the narrator speaks of what he calls 'the most frightful lament ever set up on this earth'. It is the symphonic cantata *The Lamentation of Dr Faustus*, the final musical composition of the damned Adrian Leverkühn before his pact with the devil drags him off to hell. It is a work of profound mourning, a 'dark tone-poem [that] permits up to the very end no consolation, appeasement, transfiguration'. Yet is it not conceivable, the narrator asks, 'that out of the sheerly irremediable hope might germinate?' He goes on:

> It would be but a hope beyond hopelessness, the transcendence of despair – not betrayal of it, but the miracle that passes belief. For listen to the end, listen with me: one group

of instruments after another retires, and what remains, as the work fades on the air, is the high G of a cello, the last word, the last fainting sound, slowly dying in a pianissimo-fermata. Then nothing more: silence, and night. But that tone which vibrates in the silence, which is no longer there, to which only the spirit hearkens, and which was the voice of mourning, is so no more. It changes its meaning; it abides as a light in the night.

It is not that the cantata ends on a tremulously hopeful note. On the contrary, like all pieces of music, it ends in nothing: silence. Yet this particular silence is a peculiarly palpable one, retroactively transforming the final tone of mourning into one of affirmation, and allowing it to make something new of itself in the very act of vanishing. The death of the music generates a ghostly aftermath. It is as if the cantata ends twice: once in reality, as the final note fades, and then again in the mind, the mere spectre of a sound, as something mysteriously emerges out of nothing. The last note is experienced twice, the first time as living and the second time as dead, but it is in death that it seems most alive. When the note is literally living, it is, like Faustus himself, full of grief at the prospect of its impending demise; but once it has passed into that void, it is repeated with a difference, sounding out again with a transfigured meaning. There is hope, as well as sorrow, in the fact that things pass away. Perhaps there is also hope that some unfathomable source of mercy might extend its favour even to the novel's demoniac hero, who is caught like the final note of his cantata between life and death, yet whose death-driven genius has, after all, given birth to an art in the service of the living.

Notes

Preface

1. Raymond Williams, *The Politics of Modernism* (London, 1989), 103.

1 The Banality of Optimism

1. 'The Art of Fiction', in *Henry James: Selected Literary Criticism*, ed. Morris Shapira (Harmondsworth, 1963), 97.

2. One of the few scholars to lend optimism a degree of philosophical dignity is M. A. Boden in 'Optimism', *Philosophy* 41 (1966): 291–303, an essay that reminds us that although optimism is not generally considered intellectually reputable in our own day, it was thought to be so in the eighteenth century.

3. See Erik Erikson, *Insight and Responsibility* (New York, 1994), 118.

4. See Viktor E. Frankl, *Man's Search for Meaning* (London, 2004), 140.

5. Henry James, *Literary Criticism*, vol. 2: *European Writers: Prefaces to the New York Edition* (New York, 1984), 931.

6. Walter Benjamin, *One-Way Street and Other Writings* (London, 1979), 238 (translation slightly amended).

7. See Gareth Stedman Jones, *Outcast London: A Study in the Relationship between Classes in Victorian Society* (Harmondsworth, 1976); and Marc Angenot, *Le centenaire de la Révolution 1889* (Longueuil, 1989).

8. For a (not uncritical) defence of progress and the Enlightenment, see Raymond Tallis, *Enemies of Promise* (Basingstoke, 1997).

9. Richard Swinburne, *The Existence of God* (Oxford, 1979), 219.

10. See Kenneth Surin, *Theology and the Problem of Evil* (London, 1986), 32.

11. Abolishing the future has even been advocated by some on the political left. See T. J. Clark. 'For a Left with No Future', *New Left Review*, no. 74 (March/April 2012).

12. Lionel Tiger, *The Biology of Hope* (London, 1979), 282.

13. Anthony Scioli and Henry B. Biller, *Hope in the Age of Anxiety* (Oxford, 2009), 325.

14. William James, *Pragmatism and Other Writings* (London, 2000), 129.

15. See Gabriel Marcel, *Homo Viator* (London, 1953), 34.

16. Matt Ridley, *The Rational Optimist* (London, 2011), 353. Further page references to this work will be given in parentheses after quotations.

17. For Williams's treatment of the topic, see his *The Country and the City* (London, 1973), chap. 2.

18. Quoted by Josef Pieper, *Hope and History* (London, 1969), 75.

19. T. J. Clark writes of the 'endless political and economic Micawberism' of conventional progressivist thought in 'For a Left with No Future', 72.

20. Steven Pinker, *The Better Angels of Our Nature* (London, 2011), 250.

21. Leon Trotsky, *Literature and Revolution* (New York, 1957), 254–56.

22. See Walter Benjamin, 'Theses on the Philosophy of History', in *Illuminations*, ed. Hannah Arendt (London, 1999). Peter Szondi sees a concern with 'those moments of childhood in which a token of the future lies hidden' as characteristic of Benjamin's method in his autobiography *A Berlin Childhood*. See Szondi, *On Textual Understanding* (Manchester, 1986), 154.

23. See Giorgio Agamben, *The Time That Remains: A Commentary on the Letter to the Romans* (Stanford, 2005), chap. 2.

24. Alain Badiou in Costas Douzinas and Slavoj Žižek, eds., *The Idea of Communism* (London, 2010), 10.

25. Antoine Compagnon, *The Five Paradoxes of Modernity* (New York, 1994), 44–45.

26. Quoted by Michael Lowy, *Fire Alarm: Walter Benjamin's 'On the Concept of History'* (London, 2005), 32.

27. Quoted in ibid., 84.

28. Ernst Bloch, *The Principle of Hope*, translated by Neville Plaice, Stephen Plaice, and Paul Knight, 3 vols. (Cambridge, Mass., 1995), 1:200.

29. Lowy, *Fire Alarm*, 65–66.

30. Karl Marx, *Theories of Surplus Value* (London, 1972), 134 (italics in original).

31. Fredric Jameson, *Marxism and Form* (Princeton, 1971), 134.

32. Quoted in Lowy, *Fire Alarm*, 31.

33. George Steiner, *The Death of Tragedy* (New York, 1961), 129.

34. Avery Dulles, 'An Apologetics of Hope', in *The Great Experiment: Essays in Hope*, ed. Joseph Whelan (New York, 1971), 134.

2 What is Hope?

1. George Steiner, '"Tragedy", Reconsidered', in *Rethinking Tragedy*, ed. Rita Felski (Baltimore, 2008), 40.

2. See, for example, Roger Scruton, *The Uses of Pessimism and the Danger of False Hope* (London, 2010).

3. Peter Geach, *The Virtues* (Cambridge, 1977), 48.

4. Rebecca Coleman and Debra Ferredy, eds., *Hope and Feminist Theory* (London, 2011), 16.

5. See Raymond Williams, *Modern Tragedy* (London, 1966), 59.

6. St. Augustine, *Enchiridion: On Faith, Hope, and Love* (Washington, D.C., 1996), 8.

7. Patrick Shade, *Habits of Hope* (Nashville, 2001), 70.

8. Denys Turner, *Thomas Aquinas: A Portrait* (New Haven, 2013), 161. In his *Enchiridion*, St. Augustine sees charity as presupposing hope, and both virtues as presupposing faith.

9. Erik Erikson, *Insight and Responsibility* (New York, 1994), 115 and 117.

10. Quoted by Dominic Doyle, *The Promise of Christian Humanism: Thomas Aquinas on Hope* (New York, 2011), 76. Aquinas has in mind here hope in the sense of an everyday emotion, not as a theological virtue.

11. Karl Rahner, 'On the Theology of Hope', in *Theological Investigations*, vol. 10 (New York, 1977), 254.

12. Quoted in David Nokes, *Samuel Johnson: A Life* (London, 2010), 133.

13. *The Yale Edition of the Works of Samuel Johnson*, vol. 4 (New Haven, 1969), 192.

14. Robert M. Gordon, *The Structure of Emotions* (Cambridge, 1987), 85.

15. See Gabriel Marcel, 'Desire and Hope', in *Existential Phenomenology*, ed. Nathaniel Lawrence and Daniel O'Connor (Englewood Cliffs, N.J., 1967), 280.

16. See Colin Radford and J. M. Hinton, 'Hoping and Wishing', *Proceedings of the Aristotelian Society* 44 (1970): 78.

17. For an excellent investigation of these and other questions, see James L. Muyskens, *The Sufficiency of Hope* (Philadelphia, 1979).

18. On wishing for the impossible, see J. M. O. Wheatley, 'Wishing and Hoping', *Analysis* 18, no. 6 (June 1958).

19. Paul Ricoeur, *Essays on Biblical Interpretation* (Philadelphia, 1980), 161.

20. See Stan van Hooft, *Hope* (Durham, N.C., 2011), 25.

21. See Robert Audi, *Rationality and Religious Commitment* (Oxford, 2011), 74.

22. Ibid.

23. Thomas Aquinas, *Summa Theologiae*, vol. 33 (London and New York, 1966), 7. For a brief commentary on Aquinas on hope, see Hans Urs von Balthasar, *Dare We Hope 'That All Men Be Saved'?* (San Francisco, 1988), chap. 4.

24. Aquinas, *Summa Theologiae*, vol. 33, 13.

25. Ibid., 5.

26. For a useful account of Kant on hope, see Curtis H. Peters, *Kant's Philosophy of Hope* (New York, 1993).

27. C. Peterson and Martin E. P. Seligman, *Character Strengths and Virtues: A Handbook and Classification* (Oxford, 2004), 570.

28. For Bloch's concept of noncontemporaneity, see in particular his *Heritage of Our Times* (Cambridge, 1991), part 1.

29. Ernst Bloch, *The Principle of Hope*, translated by Neville Plaice, Stephen Plaice, and Paul Knight, 3 vols. (Cambridge, Mass., 1995), 1:188.

30. Ludwig Wittgenstein, *Philosophical Investigations* (Oxford, 1983), part 2 (1), 174e.

31. I derive the information from fishermen in the village of Ross Roe in the West of Ireland, where Wittgenstein spent some time and where according to local legend he requested his neighbours to keep their dogs from barking while he was at work on the *Philosophical Investigations*.

32. See Colin Radford, 'Hoping, Wishing and Dogs', *Inquiry* 13 (Spring 1970): 100–103.

33. Quoted by Jürgen Moltmann, *Theology of Hope* (London, 1967), 35.

34. Jürgen Moltmann, 'Hoping and Planning', *Cross Currents* 18, no. 3 (Summer 1989): 310.

35. Moltmann, *Theology of Hope*, 16.

36. Wolfhart Pannenberg, 'The God of Hope', *Cross Currents* 18, no. 3 (Summer 1989): 289 and 290.

37. Paul Ricoeur, 'Hope and the Structure of Philosophical Systems', *Proceedings of the American Catholic Philosophical Association* 44 (1970): 60.

38. Nicholas Boyle, *Who Are We Now?* (Notre Dame, Ind., 1998), 178.

39. See Aristotle, *Rhetoric* (Cambridge, Mass., 1994), 117–18.

40. John Locke, *An Essay Concerning Human Understanding* (New York, 1959), 2:9.

41. See David Hume, *A Treatise of Human Nature* (Oxford, 1958), 438.

42. See J. Day, 'Hope', *American Philosophical Quarterly* 6, no. 2 (April 1969).

43. Hooft, *Hope*, 16.

44. Jayne M. Waterworth, *A Philosophical Analysis of Hope* (London, 2004), 54.

45. See Day, 'Hope', 98.

46. Aquinas, *Summa Theologiae*, vol. 33, 3.

47. John Stuart Mill, *Theism* (New York, 1957), 163.

48. Martin Luther, *What Luther Says* (St. Louis, 1959), 668.

49. Alain Badiou, *Saint Paul: The Foundation of Universalism* (Stanford, 2003), 93.

50. For a discussion of this point, see Rudolf Bultmann and Karl Heinrich Rengsdorf, *Hope* (London, 1963), 4–5.

51. Turner, *Thomas Aquinas*, 175.

52. Waterworth, *A Philosophical Analysis of Hope*, 74.

53. Hooft, *Hope*, 102.

54. Gabriel Marcel, *Homo Viator: Introduction to a Metaphysic of Hope* (London, 1951), 32. Subsequent page references to this work will be given in parentheses after quotations.

55. Josef Pieper, *On Hope* (San Francisco, 1986), 38.

56. Wayne Hudson, *The Marxist Philosophy of Ernst Bloch* (London, 1982), 108.

57. Gabriel Marcel, *The Philosophy of Existentialism* (New York, 1995), 28.

58. Andrew Benjamin, *Present Hope: Philosophy, Architecture, Judaism* (London, 1997), 128.

59. Ibid., 125.

60. Darren Webb draws a similar distinction between hope for a specific object and a more general, open-ended form of hope, which is perhaps what is meant by 'hopefulness'. See 'Modes of Hoping', *History of the Human Sciences* 20, no. 3 (2007).

61. Immanuel Kant, *Religion within the Limits of Reason Alone* (New York, 1960), 159–60. Curtis H. Peters holds that the idea of hope is far more central to Kant's thought than has generally been considered, and argues that it is in his view the main topic of the philosophy of religion. See his *Kant's Philosophy of Hope* (New York, 1993).

62. In speaking of US foreign policy, Rumsfeld differentiated between things we know and know we know, things we know we don't know, and things we don't know we don't know. He passed over a further permutation – things we know but don't know we know – which is of relevance to the theory of ideology.

63. On the obscurity of Christian hope, see Louis Dupré, 'Hope and Transcendence', in *The Great Experiment: Essays in Hope*, ed. Joseph P. Whelan (New York, 1971), 219.

64. Eric Fromm, *The Revolution of Hope* (New York, 1968), 13.

65. Fredric Jameson, *Marxism and Form* (Princeton, 1971), 155.

66. See Ludwig Feuerbach, *The Essence of Christianity* (New York, 1957), 236.

67. Fromm fails adequately to grasp the relation between faith and hope when he writes of hope as 'the mood that accompanies faith'. See *The Revolution of Hope*, 15.

68. Raymond Williams, *Culture and Society, 1780–1950* (Harmondsworth, 1985), 320.

69. Rahner, 'On the Theology of Hope', 257.

70. Ibid., 258.

71. Moltmann, *Theology of Hope*, 22.

72. John Macquarrie, *Christian Hope* (London, 1978), 27. For a useful general survey of the theology of hope, see Reuben A. Alves, *A Theology of Human Hope* (St. Meinrad, Ind., 1972).

73. Quoted in Bultmann and Rengsdorf, *Hope*, 17.

74. Søren Kierkegaard, *The Sickness Unto Death* (Harmondsworth, 1989), 92.

75. Gabriel Marcel, *Being and Having* (New York, 1965), 91.

76. Joseph J. Godfrey, *A Philosophy of Human Hope* (Dordrecht, 1987), 3 and 34.

77. John Gray, *Straw Dogs* (London, 2002), 151.

78. Day, 'Hope', 98–99.

79. Kierkegaard, *The Sickness Unto Death*, 48.

80. For more on this condition, see Terry Eagleton, *On Evil* (New Haven, 2010).

81. Kierkegaard, *The Sickness Unto Death*, 105.

82. Ibid., 88.

83. Ibid., 64.

84. See, for example, Bernard Dauenhauer, 'Hope and Politics', *Philosophy Today* 30 (Summer 1986): 93.

85. See Antoine-Nicolas de Condorcet, *Sketch for a Historical Picture of the Progress of the Human Mind* (London, 1955), 173.

86. See Badiou, *Saint Paul*, 15.

87. Jean-Luc Nancy, *Adoration: The Deconstruction of Christianity II* (New York, 2013), 88.

88. Quoted by Balthasar, *Dare We Hope?*, 87.

89. Ricoeur, 'Hope and the Structure of Philosophical Systems', 64.

90. Nicholas Lash, *A Matter of Hope: A Theologian's Reflections on the Thought of Karl Marx* (Notre Dame, Ind., 1982), 62.

91. C. S. Peirce, *Collected Papers* (Cambridge, Mass., 1965), 357.

92. Bultmann and Rengsdorf, *Hope*, 13.

93. Aquinas, *Summa Theologiae*, vol. 33, 161. The commentator is anonymous. For a scholarly account of Aquinas on hope, see Walter M. Conlon, OP, 'The Certitude of Hope (Part 1)', *The Thomist* 10, no. 1 (January 1947).

94. Shade, *Habits of Hope*, 70.

95. Erwin James, in the *Guardian* (Manchester), July 8, 2013.

96. Cicero, *On the Good Life* (London, 1971), 61.

97. Seneca, *Moral Essays* (Cambridge, Mass., 2006), 2:215.

98. Arthur Schopenhauer, *The World as Will and Representation* (New York, 1969), 1:87.

3 The Philosopher of Hope

1. Jürgen Habermas, 'Ernst Bloch – A Marxist Romantic', *Salmagundi*, nos. 10–11 (Fall 1969–Winter 1970): 316 (translation modified).

2. Ernst Bloch, *The Principle of Hope*, translated by Neville Plaice, Stephen Plaice, and Paul Knight, 3 vols. (Cambridge, Mass., 1995), 1:303 (this translation must acknowledge some responsibility for the clotted prose).

3. Quoted by David Miller, 'A Marxist Poetics', in *The Privatization of Hope: Ernst Bloch and the Future of Utopia*, ed. Peter Thompson and Slavoj Žižek (Durham, N.C., 2013), 204.

4. Vincent Geoghegan, *Ernst Bloch* (London, 1996), 4. For Bloch's Stalinism, see Oskar Negt, 'Ernst Bloch – The German Philosopher of the October Revolution', *New German Critique*, no. 4 (Winter 1975); and Jan Robert Bloch, 'How Can We Understand the Bends in the Upright Gait?', *New German Critique*, no. 35 (Fall 1988).

5. Habermas, 'Ernst Bloch', 322.

6. Perry Anderson, *Considerations on Western Marxism* (London, 1976), chap. 1.

7. Habermas, 'Ernst Bloch', 319–20.

8. Leszek Kołakowski, *Main Currents of Marxism*, vol. 2: *The Breakdown* (Oxford, 1978), 421.

9. Douglas Kellner and Harry O'Hara, 'Utopia and Marxism in Ernst Bloch', *New German Critique*, no. 9 (Fall 1976): 16.

10. The political philosopher Ronald Aronson is of this opinion. See Geoghegan, *Ernst Bloch*, 45.

11. Bloch, *The Principle of Hope*, 1:198.

12. Ibid., 1:336.

13. Ibid., 1:238.

14. Ibid., 1:196.

15. Wayne Hudson, *The Marxist Philosophy of Ernst Bloch* (London, 1982), 95.

16. Ibid., 157.

17. For a neglected but highly original study of Hardy in this respect, see Roy Morrell, *Thomas Hardy: The Will and the Way* (Kuala Lumpur, 1965).

18. Bloch, *The Principle of Hope*, 1:235.

19. See Terry Eagleton, *On Evil* (London, 2010), chap. 2.

20. The issue is well discussed in S. H. Rigby, *Marxism and History* (Manchester, 1987).

21. Fredric Jameson, *Marxism and Form* (Princeton, 1971), 133. It is not clear whether Jameson is endorsing or ventriloquising Bloch here, although it is worth pointing out that his account of his work is quite remarkably uncritical.

22. Habermas, 'Ernst Bloch', 312.

23. Jameson, *Marxism and Form*, 41.
24. Bloch, *The Principle of Hope*, 1:285.
25. Kołakowski, *Main Currents of Marxism*, vol. 2, 446.
26. Tom Moylan investigates the discrepancy between linear and non-linear conceptions of historical time in Bloch's thought in 'Bloch against Bloch: The Theological Reception of *Das Prinzip Hoffnung* and the Liberation of the Utopian Function', in *Not Yet: Reconsidering Ernst Bloch*, ed. Jamie Owen Daniel and Tom Moylan (London, 1997). It is worth noting that this useful volume of essays is scarcely able to muster a single major criticism of the *maître*. Much the same is true of another recent collection, Thompson and Žižek's *The Privatization of Hope*.
27. Bloch, *The Principle of Hope*, 1:3.
28. Ibid., 3:1358.
29. Ibid., 3:311.
30. Ibid., 3:312.
31. Ibid., 3:309.
32. Ibid.
33. Ibid., 1:1173.
34. Ibid., 3:1182.
35. Ibid., 1:288.
36. Ibid., 3:1192.

4 Hope Against Hope

1. Jonathan Lear, *Radical Hope* (Cambridge, Mass., 2006), 92.
2. Ibid., 97.
3. Ibid., 2.
4. Ibid., 83.
5. Ibid., 101.
6. Ibid., 76.
7. Stanley Cavell, *Disowning Knowledge in Seven Plays of Shakespeare* (Cambridge, 2003), 112.
8. See Quentin Meillassoux, *After Finitude* (London, 2008).
9. Quoted by Graham Harmon, *Quentin Meillassoux: Philosophy in the Making* (Edinburgh, 2011), 121.
10. Walter Stein, *Criticism as Dialogue* (Cambridge, 1969), 144.
11. Bertolt Brecht, *The Messingkauf Dialogues*, translated by John Willett (London, 1965), 47.
12. Quoted in Raymond Williams, *Modern Tragedy* (London, 1966), 176.
13. Horkheimer quoted by Michael Lowy, *Fire Alarm: Walter Benjamin's 'On the Concept of History'* (London, 2005), 83.
14. Malcolm Bull, *Anti-Nietzsche* (London, 2009), 123.
15. Paul Celan, *Collected Prose* (Manchester, 1986), 34.

16. Friedrich Nietzsche, *The Portable Nietzsche*, ed. Walter Kaufmann (New York, 1982), 125.

17. Søren Kierkegaard, *The Sickness Unto Death* (Harmondsworth, 1989), 56.

18. Ibid., 60.

19. Ibid., 74.

20. Ibid., 91.

21. Ibid., 70.

22. Viktor E. Frankl, *Man's Search for Meaning* (London, 2004), 71.

23. St. Augustine, *Enchiridion: On Faith, Hope, and Love* (Washington, D.C., 1996), 8. It is true that Augustine is right on the first count if by 'good' he means 'desired by he or she who hopes'.

24. Slavoj Žižek, *Living in the End Times* (London, 2010), xiv–xv.

25. Quoted by Peter Szondi, *An Essay on the Tragic* (Stanford, 2002), 8.

26. Theodor Adorno, *Minima Moralia* (London, 1974), 227.

27. Quoted in Peter Thompson and Slavoj Žižek, eds., *The Privatization of Hope: Ernst Bloch and the Future of Utopia* (Durham, N.C., 2013), 91.

28. Quoted in Alberto Toscano, *Fanaticism* (London, 2010), 244.

29. Herbert McCabe, *Hope* (London, 1987), 15.

30. Raymond Williams, *The Politics of Modernism* (London, 1989), 104.

31. See Steven Pinker, *The Better Angels of Our Nature* (London, 2011), chap. 2. Pinker's book is my source for the other historical events recorded here.

32. Erik Erikson, *Insight and Responsibility* (New York, 1994), 118.

Index

Abraham, 49, 65, 72, 81, 113, 129
Adorno, Theodor, 5, 91, 92, 131
Aeneid (Virgil), 86
Aeschylus, 39–40, 45
Agamben, Giorgio, 28
Althusser, Louis, 79, 92
Anderson, Perry, 90, 92, 94
'An die Nachgeborenen' (Brecht), 132
animals, hope in, 53–54
Antony and Cleopatra (Shakespeare), 87, 88–89
apocalypticism, 28, 38
Aquinas, Thomas: on discomfort of hope, 52; on false aspirations, 60; on goodness of Being, 76; on hope and certainty, 82–83; on hope as future-oriented, 50, 51; on hope as virtue, 58; on hope in animals, 54; on hope struggling to attain future good, 84; on hoping for the impossible, 50; scepticism regarding hope, 43; on the theological virtues, 41–42, 57; on *voluntas*, 61
Aristotle, 51, 55, 86, 98, 132
art, 13, 32, 52, 104, 125–26
'Art of Fiction, The' (James), 1

artworks, 13, 32, 52
ataraxy, 86
atheism, 13, 98, 100, 120
Audi, Robert, 49
Augustine, St, 41, 51, 58, 83, 129–30
Austen, Jane, 14, 82
Auster, Paul, 46–47

Badiou, Alain, 28–29, 38, 59, 80
Barthes, Roland, 122
Baudelaire, Charles, 128
Beckett, Samuel, 95, 122
Benjamin, Andrew, 65
Benjamin, Walter: on Angel of History, 31, 34; aphoristic style of, 91; on artworks, 33; on belief that history is on our side, 100; considers himself beyond redemption in the present, 29–30; on hastening arrival of the Messiah, 30–31; on historical immanence of hope, 33–34; on Kant's vision of unending progress, 32; leftist historicism opposed by, 37, 106; on meaning of the past, 32–33; Messianism of, 96, 132; on nostalgia, 33; pessimism of, 5–6;